GIVE
HER
CREDIT

GIVE HER CREDIT

THE UNTOLD ACCOUNT OF A WOMEN'S BANK THAT EMPOWERED A GENERATION

Grace L. Williams

Little
a

Published by Little A, New York

www.apub.com

Amazon, the Amazon logo, and Little A are trademarks of Amazon.com, Inc., or its affiliates.

ISBN-13: 9781542025508 (hardcover)
ISBN-13: 9781542025515 (paperback)
ISBN-13: 9781542025478 (digital)

Cover design by Olga Grlic
Cover images: © 3DMI, © Bukhta Yurii, © Sammy33 / Shutterstock; © J Studios, © subjug / Getty

Printed in the United States of America

First edition

To the village that raised this writer. In particular, to Mimmy, who saw this coming long ago and reminded me to keep going and believing in the moments I forgot. And to Fred Shier, who I hope is smiling on this moment as this dedication to him is a long-ago promise kept by an eighth grader he believed in.

A NOTE FROM THE AUTHOR

This book is based on research and interviews conducted over seven years. Some names and details have been changed. The rest is written as remembered by the many people who made this bank happen and supported by documents from the time.

Contents

PROLOGUE

Denver, Colorado
Late Summer / Early Fall 1978

Mary Eckels was in a $20,000 bind.

It was 1978, four years after major legislation had given women access to lines of credit without a male guarantor, and Mary was hoping to join ranks with the roughly 1.9 million women who ran a business.

She was thirty but still coltish, with long, light-brown hair and sparkly blue eyes. She'd lived in Denver since she was three, save for the stints she'd spent farther west in California and then in New Mexico. It had been eight years since her first day as an apprentice at Gusterman Silversmiths, a shop located in the now-trendy Larimer Square section of downtown Denver.

Gusterman Silversmiths was a cheery shop within a quaint suite of brick buildings that resembled a village. Customers often came in search of a custom-designed gold or silver item or to get a ring resized or have a loose gem reset. Its founders, Stig and Astrid Gusterman, made their passage from Sweden to Colorado with their two daughters in the 1950s. Although Stig opened the shop, women ended up running it. After his sudden accidental death in the 1960s left Astrid widowed, she kept the business going. By 1970, when Mary started working there, Astrid and the other staff members were happy to teach her every aspect of the business, which Mary excelled at. By now, she could pretty much do everything in that shop.

Everything except for the management and bookkeeping.

Her lack of experience in those departments didn't affect her day-to-day at Gusterman's, but a new owner was needed. Astrid's now-grown daughters didn't want to run the Denver shop; Mary, who hailed from a family of artists and enjoyed working with stones, gems, and metals, was a natural choice. If she could come up with $20,000, she'd been told, the family would carry the note over, a sales practice that allowed her, as the buyer, to use profits from the business to pay back the loan.

All she needed to get started was a heap of money—$20,000 she didn't have. The next logical place to look was a bank.

Mary had gone to three local banks to plead her case, saying that the Gusterman family had offered to carry the note but she didn't have the $20,000 to cover her obligation. Owning a business came with challenges, but Mary found it an exciting prospect. After all, Denver was a place where, just a few generations before, plenty of adventurers had come in droves to mine for gold and silver in search of their own fortunes.

Although the mining frenzy had cooled some by the time Mary stepped inside that first bank building, metal smithing remained a respectable, promising career. Whether the economy boomed or busted, people still needed that occasional customized piece to add to a collection or some simple service like a ring resize. Gusterman's had proved this with its fifteen-year run in Larimer Square. In fact, just two years prior, the shop had expanded and moved into a bigger space within the same suite of buildings.

At the first bank, Mary shared her situation. With nothing remarkable to offer as collateral and her car as her only asset, the chance of getting any help was slim, but she still had hope.

"You have no idea what you are talking about," a well-dressed, tight-lipped man across the table had said curtly. "Go away."

In disbelief, Mary next appealed to her own bank. Surely her relationship there would result in a more productive conversation. They had their own paper trail together. They *knew* her.

If it was even possible, that meeting had gone worse. Not only had she been told she had no idea what she was talking about by another well-dressed, tight-lipped man, she'd then been sized up and advised to "go home and have children."

Having children wasn't on her immediate agenda. She certainly wasn't going to go home. She was going to somehow find a lender to help her out.

With its storied buildings, Denver's Seventeenth Street represented the beating heart of the city's financial district. It lay just a handful of walkable blocks from her shop. But it might as well have been on an entirely different planet—the cheery mom-and-pop shops were replaced with stern-looking financial buildings. Mary took a deep breath, approached a third bank, and was turned down yet again. Still, Mary wasn't about to give up.

A few weeks earlier, the opening of a different kind of bank had splashed across local headlines. It had even made some national headlines. Located in Denver's Equitable Building, at the corner of Seventeenth and Stout Streets, it was part of the fabric of Denver finance. Like any bank out there, its primary goal was to be a bank that provided services and stayed financially sound, but its name, Women's Bank, NA, signaled a significant difference from the dozens of by-men, for-men banks in Denver, three of which had already turned Mary down.

In articles about the bank prior to its opening, journalists remarked extensively about its management, which included Bessie "B." LaRae Orullian, who'd been the highest-ranking female bank officer at a male-run bank in town before joining Women's Bank, and Judith Foster, a registered investment advisor with her own advisory business. In addresses to the media, they made their mission clear: Women's Bank would operate like others on Seventeenth Street, with one caveat—women and other traditionally underserved clients would be met with the same opportunities and treatment usually reserved for men. They would at least be given a chance. The Women's Bank had also gotten support and mentorship from East Coast banking bigwigs like Mary Roebling, who, in 1958, was the first woman to become a governor of the American Stock Exchange.

In 1974, bank discrimination on the basis of sex had been going on rather unremarkably until a few activists pointed out its flaws. It had finally been outlawed by the passage of the Equal Credit Opportunity Act, also called "Regulation B." Yet some established banks throughout the country, including those in Denver that Mary Eckels had approached four years later, remained set in their ways. On paper, it might have been against the law to discriminate, but banks still regularly treated women unfairly. The individuals who had joined forces to open Women's Bank had borne firsthand witness to this continued unfair treatment. They had tired of waiting on the finance boy's club to adhere to the new banking and credit laws and had grown impatient for the equal access they were entitled to.

In March 1976, the founders of Women's Bank, also known as the Women's Association, had formally announced their application to organize a nationally chartered bank. Over the two-plus years it took for them to finally open to the public, plenty of buzz about their bank had built. From the outset, Women's Bank was seen as welcoming and friendly, an accessible operation. Prior to its opening, bank representatives conducted outreach to the community through speaking engagements, offering women who worked in the downtown area free brown-bag lunchtime seminars to educate them about banking and building credit.

Starting with New York City in late 1975, other women's banks had sprouted up across the US. Although some so-called experts dismissed the women's movement in banking as a passing fad or something related to the "libber mentality" sweeping the nation, something lasting stuck. Something *else*. Not since World War II had more women worked outside the home, driving demand for banks that would not only cash their checks or store their savings but also take them seriously and give them their rightful and now lawful access to credit.

Charter applications requesting permission to organize sister banks peppered legislative offices on both coasts. But Denver? Everyone in the know viewed it as the outlier in the banking sisterhood. Perhaps unfairly stereotyped for its Wild West image and "cowboy" culture, its strong position in finance went largely unremarked. Denver might have been a boomtown with robust industries in cattle, energy, and mining, but it remained overshadowed by the New York and San Francisco markets.

The opening of Women's Bank was unlike anything Denver had ever seen. Several days of celebration included taking the building's dingy alley and transforming it into a clean, bright, sparkling outdoor party space complete with food, drinks, dancing, and live music. In a very short span of time, Women's Bank had shown its spirit of welcome and empowerment, not just for women but for all of Denver, just as the Women's Association and its fifty bank founders intended.

Antidiscrimination practices may have been the law on the books, but four years after the law had passed, Mary Eckels was still struggling to have a simple conversation about a loan. Not only had she struck out at three banks, including her own, but she had been advised to go home and have children instead of becoming an entrepreneur—arguably, advice that fell outside the expertise of the bank in question. But Mary *wanted* to step into the ownership role at the shop and therefore needed the money to buy it. Like most anyone in town by then, she had probably seen the advertisements for Women's Bank that included the bespoke phone number (303) 293-BANK.

What did she have to lose by trying the Women's Bank? The fact that it was located in the Equitable Building might have even seemed like a good omen. On the day she walked into the narrow hallway and up to the teller area, she paused, taking a moment to absorb it all.

The space was smaller than that of other banks, but it was clear that great pains had been taken to transform it into a place where everyone felt welcome. In lieu of the dark wood that adorned other banks, the walls of the Women's Bank were painted a warm, golden yellow. Local artists' works hung on the walls in a rotating exhibit, and individual teller windows were removed. Instead, tellers stood at open countertops, facing bank clients directly, thus eliminating the traditional barrier between client and teller. Smartly dressed staff commingled with one another.

It just felt *different* in there.

"How can we help you?"

Mary Eckels looked up. With the last bit of hope in her heart, she began to state her case for the fourth time. She'd been in the same job at an established local business for nearly a decade. Now she'd been given the opportunity to buy it for $20,000 she didn't have. The teller waved for a loan officer to come over, and before she realized it, Mary found herself repeating her story.

The woman facing her was professionally dressed, yet somehow not like the stodgy men she had encountered up and down Seventeenth Street. The woman wasn't curt or impossible in their exchanges, either. Mary remembers her as being extra kind in that moment. She had listened to her and hadn't said anything discouraging. Instead, she'd nodded as if to say "go on."

Mary didn't have any assets, save for her car. Could they help her?

The woman smiled warmly. "We can't go against sound banking practices here," she explained. "Do you know what that means?"

Mary nodded glumly. She had an idea.

"Although I can't loan you the money today, Mary, I can still help you figure out how to make this work."

Mary exhaled. Nobody else had offered her so much as a glass of water or a complimentary pen up to now. But this woman at this bank was willing to help her try to secure her loan.

Finally, she had come to the right place.

CHAPTER 1

How the West Was Hers

A long, long time ago and once upon a time . . .

One of the first nationally chartered women's banks was founded in Colorado. Locales like New York, or Chicago, or San Francisco might have been more expected to break that ground. However, to anyone who knows their western history, it's probably not a surprise that Colorado was among the states that led the way. Despite that Wild West image, the western lands that would later become Colorado had a history of being friendlier toward women, even before the nation's founding.

Prior to the Louisiana Purchase of 1803, the territory had been under Spanish rule during the 1700s, rather than under British rule like in the east. Spanish rule gave women in America the same rights afforded to women in Spain. When it came to property rights, Spanish law transcended gender. By default, this rule also applied to North American women living within Spanish territory as far back as the 1500s and 1600s. In the 1840s, some changes to these laws favored the property rights of men over those of women. The newer laws were closer to those in the east, but in the Wild West, a large subset of American women still enjoyed the right to property.

While the sisterhood back east struggled to gain recognition as individuals, including securing the right to vote, western states were also the first to understand and protect the importance of women exercising their rights and autonomy. Women's suffrage was granted out west decades ahead of its national adoption. On December 10, 1869, the Wyoming Territory granted women the right to vote, and in 1870, women in Utah gained the right to vote.

In Colorado, women attained voting rights at a referendum on women's suffrage held on November 7, 1893. Getting there had taken years of careful organizing, plan revision, and waiting. Support from elected officials stretched as far back as 1868, when former territorial governor John Evans came out publicly in favor of women's suffrage. Two years later, Governor Edward McCook declared that universal suffrage was "an inevitable result of progressive civilization."

Populists, who came into political power in 1892 after the economy had cratered, thought they'd steady Colorado by supporting more labor unions and farming, an eight-hour workday, a return to the silver standard, and anti-monopoly legislation. Importantly, they said, "Let the women vote, they can't do any worse than the men."

"Can't do any worse than the men" is a common thread when it comes to the story of women attaining their rights in the US. It stretches into matters of finance too.

In Colorado, suffrage passed by over six thousand votes. Upon learning of their victory, suffragettes and supporters gathered at their headquarters to celebrate, where they poured into the streets singing the hymn "Praise God from Whom All Blessings Flow" in unison.

The campaign for women's suffrage in America is rightly associated with Elizabeth Cady Stanton and Susan B. Anthony. Yet those august women, as New Yorkers, were not able to vote in their lifetimes, as their state didn't grant women the right to vote until 1917. The Wild West may bring to mind cowboys, vast skies, and a certain lawlessness. But it should also be recognized for adopting the "wild" idea that women deserved to own property and vote long before the east caught up.

And in the case of Denver and its women's bank, the story begins, ironically, with a western-raised woman heading to her new life, which happened to lay eastward in proximity to her hometown.

CHAPTER 2

LaRae

Messenger Girl, Age 18 to 23
Credit experience helpful, good appearance and personality. Women with children under 12 yrs. need not apply. Apply in person.
—From a want ad in the *Salt Lake Tribune*, May 13, 1952

Summer 1954

For nearly two centuries, travelers shuffling from one North American coast to the other have encountered the former prairie trail we now know as Interstate 80. It is nearly three thousand miles long, stretching from San Francisco, California, to Teaneck, New Jersey, etching a blacktopped lifeline across the nation's palm. On the map, the interstate dips and rises, bumping up against intersecting cities and communities, giving road trippers the experience of a thriving, diverse expanse known as "the heartland."

For those who prefer to live on the coasts or to travel by air, however, this stretch of land sometimes gets a different designation: "flyover country," a place to be avoided while en route elsewhere. But to label it "flyover country" or dismiss it outright is unkind to its history, square miles, and the people who continue to make it their home. "Flyover country" mutes the majesty and denies the homage owed to the mountains, valleys, deserts, rivers, prairie, grainfields, and cow pastures still encountered to this day by car window.

The beginnings of Interstate 80—then called the Lincoln Highway—traveled alongside another important pathway of historical significance, the Mormon Trail. From 1846 onward, Mormon pioneers traveled it from east to west, escaping religious persecution in Illinois to search for their promised land. The pioneer trail stops in what is today's Salt Lake City, Utah, the state's capital and its best-known Mormon settlement.

By 1954, the smooth, now-paved routes, which had yet to become commissioned highways, served a different purpose for one Mormon girl that year.

That was the summer when twenty-one-year-old B. LaRae Orullian found herself sitting in the driver's seat of her swanky green 1949 Ford, eastward bound. She had saved up to buy that car with cash because, in those days, a woman who needed financing for anything, including a car, would need a man to sign his name alongside hers in a sort of vouching system that persisted.

She was cutting her way across the Rocky Mountains, which had been the scenic backdrop of Salt Lake City, where she had grown up. She was choosing herself, heading in the exact opposite direction that her pioneer ancestors had traveled so long ago.

LaRae and her Ford had found their way out of Salt Lake City and on to new opportunities.

The road stretched in a V around her, with a sense of possibility hanging in the air up ahead and the life she had just left behind barely concluded. Her more than five-hundred-mile trip to Denver was a drive toward her future and the adventure she was determined to have.

That year, as Rosemary Clooney crooned "Hey There" on the radio, a peaches-and-cream life seemed predestined for girls in LaRae's age group, Mormon or otherwise. All they had to do was trust in a prefabricated formula: Find a man and fall in love. Get married and have babies. *But,* she couldn't help wondering, *perhaps there might be options out there that had to do with other things and different roads to follow. Try not to think of the life you had before. Think about an exciting future ahead.*

The Great Unknown presented itself in cinematic Technicolor when it smiled outward to young onlookers. From the pages of glossy magazines and department store catalogs, the gray doldrums of the Great Depression and the war years appeared to have been transformed. In their place was the sparkling, bright here and now—which felt like when Dorothy first opens the front door of her family farmhouse, stepping out of the black-and-white world of Kansas and into the colorful, wonderful land of Oz. The many shiny fixtures and trims and the promise of a lack for nothing seemed to ask, *What could possibly go wrong?* LaRae, too, felt the endless possibilities of whatever door she was about to open. Her clear, sky-blue eyes scanned the roadway. This same road would one day, she hoped, bring her straight into New York City, where she would work on Wall Street. But Denver was going to be the first stop on her journey. She had no idea who or what she might eventually become. But she did know that in matters of love, family, and romance, whatever the other girls back home were buying right now probably wasn't for her.

Throughout LaRae's generation, a popular trend had unfolded. Some women had been to college or worked steady jobs during the war, but joining the smiling faces in Technicolor land meant those days were over. Sure, maybe you liked to paint or had traveled to Paris, but what did it matter in the long run?

"Just play along, little sisters," the sweet Technicolor message coaxed seductively, "and riches shall be your reward. A man will take good care of you. Simply turn in your ticket and find out."

Catalogs and houses were pretty, but their promises had somehow lost some of their shine for LaRae. As she eased the steering wheel, bringing the car around curves and keeping it moving between the road's painted lines, she had a lot to contend with. By leaving, she had just openly chosen to follow a different pathway, one that took her out of her community and away from her friends and family.

Always the dutiful daughter who respected rules and traditions, in that moment she had caused a kerfuffle. LaRae had broken off a long engagement to a perfectly decent young man. And then, with her community and family still reeling, she had packed up and left. Glancing in the rearview mirror from time to time, she understood that her actions in Salt Lake had left a trail of heartbreak behind her. There were heartbroken parents and a heartbroken ex-fiancé, and of course, his heartbroken family completed the sad circle she'd created. It hadn't been easy for her to make the choice to leave either. If she was being truthful with herself, she couldn't deny it was one of the hardest decisions she'd had to make in her twenty-one years of life.

LaRae also hadn't intentionally set out to upset her family and hadn't imagined she'd hurt anyone. She loved her family and community, she adored her parents. Growing up in the Latter-day Saints Church, she experienced what most regarded as the ideal Mormon home life and upbringing. Her parents had modeled the examples of a hardworking father as the primary breadwinner and a stay-at-home mother raising the four Orullian children.

Like most families around them, they lived happily practicing modesty, service, and thrift in both the community and at home. Sometimes— it felt like yesterday—she had tagged along with her two sisters and brother to the grocer, where every paper-wrapped, string-tied meat purchase netted the family both something to eat and the excitement of a brand-new bit of string. The paper around the meat was discarded, but the string that tied it never went to waste. Instead, it ended up as an addition to a never-ending string ball the Orullians used for other projects.

At nine, LaRae learned how to scale cherry trees and shimmy far enough out on their limbs to pick the red, ripe fruits growing there, which she'd later sell. A seasonal career in picking strawberries soon followed.

As she grew older, her parents encouraged her to be competitive, to play basketball and softball. They often encouraged her to enjoy her leisure time, but LaRae also understood the importance of working to earn and save her own money. Her work ethic landed her a steady stream of jobs, including one with a family with five children who lived across town. This assignment meant a bicycle commute to manage a houseful of children and tasks like doing their laundry and ironing (which she loathed), but just the mere possibility of a twenty-dollar-per-week salary was incentive enough to more than pique her interest.

In the seventh grade, her sharpness and savvy garnered the attention of her science teacher, who planted a seed in the girl's head, telling her she had a good business mind. "You need to be a businesswoman," the teacher had said. But what kind of business opportunities existed for a girl back in the 1940s and 1950s? Most careers outside of the home were in teaching or nursing. Businesswomen were rare finds, indeed.

Growing up, LaRae had been editor of her school paper and had considered a journalism career or maybe teaching, but she'd also envisioned a future in law or engineering. A partial scholarship to Brigham Young University had meant she needed to find work to offset the tuition, and two opportunities had presented themselves. LaRae could proof entries in the upcoming edition of the phone book, or she could apply to be a bank messenger girl.

She'd chosen the job as a messenger girl for a local bank, the Tracy Collins Bank and Trust. She was tall, with a head of stylish, dark hair that made her bright eyes stand out. She possessed a firm but soothing voice and easily joked with friends that the "B" in her given name, Bessie, which she had abbreviated, actually stood for "big, bossy babe."

Over time, her participation in both basketball and softball had provided her with a robust, strong physique that she wasn't afraid to dress in a comfortable but modern wardrobe of dresses, sweaters, skirts, and blouses, so long as the uniform remained modest.

At Tracy Collins, the messenger girls were on hand to assist with whatever was needed. Tasks intertwined and changed daily but often meant running countless errands and making oneself indispensable and useful to the bank. Sometimes, they'd step out to a nearby bakery to pick out boxes of still-warm doughnuts for the office workers to enjoy. In addition to doughnuts, messenger girls also put out the day's desserts for everyone. Other times, they ran deposits from their worksite to other locations. The messenger girls with experience usually trained the newbies, and together, they tackled their collective duties.

Early on, LaRae had shown her talent for the job. She knew both the staff members and the opening and closing schedules of necessary entities like the post office. She had also figured out the quickest routes to get her to and from Tracy Collins and other locations around Salt Lake.

She was a mere handful of weeks into her work as a messenger girl when her supervisors pulled her aside. They had some pretty good news for LaRae. They'd noticed how well she had taken to her job. If she was willing, they'd like to promote her to the role of coin wrapper. Would she accept the move?

She would. And to master her coin-wrapping duties, LaRae memorized the sensation and heft of exactly fifty cool, shiny pennies in her palm. This muscle memory enabled her to weigh and slide the pennies into their corresponding stiff paper wrappers using just her hands and to entirely bypass the extra steps and time it took to individually count the coins. Once she had streamlined coin wrapping, she figured out how to make the process go even faster. From then onward, her supervisors rewarded her ambition with a series of promotions—first to file clerk, where she handled the bank's loan documents, and then to typist, where she prepared them.

Around that same time, LaRae began a slow transition toward another promotion of sorts—to that of "future Mrs." While she was still in her late teens, that perfectly decent young man from her community had proposed. There was a caveat, though. He had asked for her hand in marriage before setting off for a two-year mission to England. His departure meant she would have to wait for him. Would she?

Young LaRae had said yes, she would wait for him.

The pair agreed on a June wedding. It was to take place as soon as he returned home. LaRae would be just a month past her twenty-first birthday. Meanwhile, amid the details and steps it took to plan her wedding—the debates over an organza versus taffeta dress or the fretting about what food to serve to guests—another dilemma inserted itself right into the middle of her life.

Tracy Collins Bank and Trust promoted her. *Again.*

Eventually, the former messenger girl found herself running the department handling Federal Housing Administration Title 1 loans, where she learned to make government-insured loans on the bank's behalf. Banks, it turned out, fascinated her, and the deep-down truth was that she really enjoyed her work at that bank.

Part of her fascination included plenty of stops to admire the section of the building she had nicknamed "Mahogany Row." Sometimes, when it was quiet, or the moment seized her fancy, she would slip from her desk and cross the floor over to Mahogany Row. This was where the bank's all-male management staff kept their offices and held important meetings. Mahogany Row had beautiful, sturdy dark-wood furniture and fine-looking artwork hung on its walls.

There were no women executives on Mahogany Row, but still, LaRae Orullian held out a bit of hope for herself. *Someday. Someday, I could have a seat here too,* she'd think, admiring the furnishings and whom they represented. *Someday, I will be a part of Mahogany Row. I will have an office with fine, dark wood and the artwork of my choosing on its walls.* Even as her ambitions called out to her, the wise words of one colleague stuck in her mind. If one wanted to get anywhere at the bank, she'd said, they needed to get into commercial lending. But all of the commercial lenders at that time were men.

Just like all of Mahogany Row.

With the idea of getting to Mahogany Row steadily gnawing at her, LaRae felt herself pulled in two different directions. She was raised by a family that prized women who prized the Mormon ideal of getting married and folding into family and community commitments. How many of her friends were also preparing to become that ideal? How many weddings had she attended or even stood in as a bridesmaid? Conventional wisdom would have her following the plan set before her. Make a choice:

pick a chicken dish, choose organza or taffeta, get married, have babies. Perhaps she should not have let her mind wander so much toward thinking of how to get a seat on Mahogany Row. For a woman, it was risky.

And yet, as she celebrated her twenty-first birthday in May and as her expected June 2 wedding date loomed, a sinking feeling came over her during daily activities, like while she dressed for work in the mornings. LaRae knew that if she went through with the wedding, her life at the bank must eventually come to an end. There was no other choice. Even the want ads made it pretty clear in their postings. Some messenger girl jobs would only allow applicants to have children over the age of twelve. If she had any babies, by the time they were twelve and she could reapply, she would be over the hiring-age limit of twenty-three and well into her thirties, possibly even in her forties. Following the ideal left no room to get her that hoped-for seat on Mahogany Row.

Though her impending choice was always lurking in her mind, LaRae had still followed through with most of her preparations. After her fiancé's return two years later, however, her thoughts about the future, specifically hers, had changed. On the day he returned, she had somewhat reluctantly accompanied his family to the train station to retrieve him.

That day, as she rode to the train station with his family, it was possible that she felt walls closing in on her. Could she accept the ultimatum and choose him? Would she take a deep breath, join the happy faces with perfect lives in the Technicolor land, and let this man be her life now? He'd seemed so confident about wanting it. Her friends seemed so confident about wanting it too. Would she? Could children and a life as his wife be enough for her after all? There was nothing wrong with choosing a life as a wife and mother. But couldn't it also be fine to want a career, even if it was a bit more unconventional? The moment he stepped from the train and their eyes met, the answer hit her almost as if she had been struck by a train. It stopped her cold.

LaRae decided she would not marry him. Instead, she would seek this pathway in a Wild West adventure of her own; she was going to become a businesswoman.

CHAPTER 3

Laws Are Not Enough

In 1963, when President John F. Kennedy signed the Equal Pay Act into law, the goal was that women who worked outside the home would finally receive equal pay for equal work. Equal pay meant wages for men and women doing the same jobs would match. Part of the reason for championing the law in the first place was to eliminate some of the demonstrable negative impacts that financial and sexual discrimination had on the workforce.

The administration knew, for instance, that discrimination hampered the utilization of available labor resources and led to labor disputes and unfair competition. Equal pay, they hoped, would put an end to the issues. Yet a study released in 1976 by the US Department of Labor's Women's Bureau found that, in 1974, women working outside the home full time earned a paltry fifty-seven cents on the dollar when compared to what their male counterparts earned. In the long run, this meant that, on average, women had to work nine days to achieve the same earnings that men grossed working the same job for just five days. Despite being the law, equal pay had yet to be implemented.

From 1952 to 1976, Representative Leonor K. Sullivan, a Democrat from Missouri, was agitating on behalf of the rights of consumers, a disproportionate number of whom were women. After all, women did most of the household shopping. Women priced things like the cost of a gallon of gas or quart of milk and could often be found clipping the coupons that saved them money at the grocer's. Sullivan understood the importance of standing up for women and was willing to make sure they weren't left behind with outdated laws and archaic policies. She was the first congresswoman to hold a seat in Missouri, following the death of her husband, who had previously held it. Over time, she became a respected politician with substantial legislation under her belt, notably the Food Stamp Acts of 1959 and 1964. She brought legislation to the floor that included a policy ensuring the safety of cosmetics and that their ingredients were listed on the outside of the package. Sullivan also set her sights on an issue that impacted millions of women every day: faulty pantyhose. By 1970, most working women paid what has become known as a "pink tax." Back then, it included constantly buying and replacing a steady stream of pantyhose. Unless she was wearing trousers, a professional, respectable woman didn't leave home without pantyhose on. But from a consumer standpoint, pantyhose were a colossal nightmare. They were costly and fragile.

Sullivan took on weak pantyhose, entering into the record her less-than-encouraging correspondence with officials at the National Science Foundation who perhaps didn't share her same concern about the matter. Addressing reporters, Sullivan did not let up. As quoted by United Press International (UPI) and in news sources nationwide, she said, "Millions of American women would like to see the nation which can dress men in the garments necessary to withstand the hostile environment of the moon help women to get through a day without a bag, sag, wrinkle or tear in an expensive and frequently essential article of wearing apparel here on earth." Although her war on weak pantyhose was not official congressional-rep business, per se, women everywhere could appreciate her for taking up that cause.

Sullivan had taken on food stamps, cosmetics, and pantyhose before she set her sights on equalizing the playing fields in finance and credit. Before Sullivan's groundbreaking Equal Credit Opportunity

Act in 1974, President Lyndon B. Johnson had signed the Truth in Lending Act (TILA), a precursor, in 1968 as part of the newly established Consumer Credit Protection Act. Under TILA, creditors and lenders were required by law to disclose the terms and conditions of their loans and credit to consumers. Prior to TILA's passage, states had individual sets of laws or rules about credit disclosure, a move that one expert referred to as "a hodgepodge" in an essay examining the new law and its impact. Under TILA, which also created the Uniform Consumer Credit Code, consumers now had the right to access and request specifics, such as interest rate information or repayment implications for their accounts. With these clarifications, the hope was that consumers would no longer be confused or misled about the true costs of borrowing money, since interest rates, annual percentage rates, fees, and taxes now had to be disclosed by law. Moreover, consumers could go comparison shopping among creditors to see who offered the best rate.

Lenders, perhaps understandably and perhaps out of fear of the potential competition that clear disclosure could bring, protested the act, but it passed anyway. TILA went into effect on July 1, 1969.

Sullivan championed the Equal Credit Opportunity Act because consumers, especially women, were expected to benefit from it. Also known as "Regulation B," it was first presented on Capitol Hill in 1972 as part of the National Commission on Consumer Finance hearings held on May 22 and 23. Two years later, in May 1974, Sullivan introduced the bill to the Subcommittee on Consumer Affairs of the House Banking and Currency Committee during another two-day hearing.

On the surface, Regulation B was seen as a departure for the congresswoman, as it had little to do with lipstick or pantyhose, but it did have something in common with them: it pertained to consumers, which included women.

Prior to the hearings, the National Commission on Consumer Finance released a report outlining issues that women faced around their individual access to credit. The report found that

- single women had more trouble getting credit than single men, especially credit for mortgages;
- creditors were typically not willing to extend credit to married women in their own names;
- after a woman married, a creditor could require her to reapply for credit, and it usually had to be in her husband's name;
- creditors did not have to count the wife's income if married couples applied for credit;
- divorced or widowed women faced obstacles reestablishing their own, individual credit.

Before passage of Regulation B, financial institutions were permitted to discriminate against customers based on factors such as their religion, gender, or marital status. In response to these unfair, sexist lending practices, Regulation B would make it illegal for banks, creditors, and financial institutions to refuse women the same financial privileges afforded to men. Unfortunately, despite the reach of Regulation B, religion was still one factor that was used to discriminate against consumers, causing Sullivan to declare the law not strong enough.

Proponents of Regulation B urged lawmakers to consider the life women were forced to accept when frozen out of the financial systems. Without Regulation B, they argued, creditors could abuse their positions of power and exercise carte blanche toward female applicants that was both uncomfortable and oppressive. It was standard practice, for instance, for a creditor or lender to expect access to women's personal information, such as whether she planned to have children and what kind of birth control she used, questions that were wildly inappropriate and had nothing to do with the actual credit worthiness of the woman inquiring about credit or an account. Something as simple as a telephone number on the application that was in a woman's own name, rather than a man's, could allow the creditor to refuse it.

Being married, using the title Mrs. with a man's first and last name, or even using a man's surname in the white pages was not a cure-all for women seeking out credit. A creditor could also legally ask a married couple about their birth-control choices and further probe into the particularities of what method they were using. As many couples had learned regarding their mortgage, if the wife was considered "of child-bearing age," the woman's contribution to the couple's finances would often be completely ignored.

Some lenders required couples to present them with a "baby letter" from their doctor. This invasive document verified such personal information as the confirmation that one party within the couple was sterile or that they were prescribed reliable birth control. It could also tell the lender that the doctor was willing to terminate a pregnancy if needed. Regarding any living children in the family, a creditor could ask the couple about what childcare arrangements were in place and if college was in the cards for the children.

Perhaps most astonishing and frustrating was that even after all of this invasive, irrelevant information had been disclosed to a lender, bank, or creditor, the wife's income could still be discounted or entirely uncounted by the financial institution. This refusal was easily justified by creditors because of an assumption that women's income was "pin money" or temporary income, at best. In the lenders' minds, all women would eventually quit their jobs and assume their "proper" place in the home raising children and tending to housework. The wife's income, therefore, could not be counted as a reliable indicator of what loan terms, amounts, and interest rates a couple qualified for together.

In addition to the other egregious and unfair practices it took aim at, Regulation B sought to end the practice by institutions of assigning monetary value to a woman based on her marital status. It went so far as to discourage the act of abusing courtesy titles such as Miss or Mrs. to deter potential and current applicants. If a woman was divorced, institutions could label alimony and support payments as unreliable income sources. One had to wonder, if an ex-husband was considered unreliable, did that impact *his* ability to apply for credit? The presumed answer was always and forever no. It didn't. Of course not, because he was a man.

In July 1975, as reported in the *Congressional Record*, Sullivan testified before the Subcommittee on Consumer Affairs:

> Title V of the Public Law 93-495 created the Equal Credit Opportunity Act of 1974 which takes effect exactly 15 weeks from today. This Senate measure, on which there were also no Senate hearings, disregarded the information developed in comprehensive House hearings on the scope of credit discrimination. It is a weak and abbreviated version of a much stronger House bill which was bypassed and buried in a series of parliamentary maneuvers which were, to say the least, unfortunate for the consumers. Fortunately, all of the good provisions of last year's House bill, H.R. 14856, plus some improvements which I support, are included in S. 1927—a better bill than the one passed by the House this year as H.R. 6516. The Equal Credit Opportunity Act, as I said, will take effect in 15 weeks, will undoubtedly help many women, and men, too, who are creditworthy and who happen to be single, divorced, separated or widowed, in overcoming traditional and often irrational discriminations in the credit market—but it will help mainly those who are native whites between the ages of 26 and, say, 55. It has a ceiling on punitive damages in class actions of the lesser of $100,000 or 1% of a creditor's net worth. It does not cover discrimination based on race, color, religion, national origin, or age—all of which are covered by the House-passed H.R. 6516 and by S. 1927. The hearings of my Subcommittee in the last Congress clearly established the need for such broadened coverage. Ostensibly a "women's" law, the Equal Credit Opportunity Act of 1974 does nothing for the woman who happens to be black, or Spanish-speaking, or Indian, or under 26 or over 55, or for men, either, in those categories.

CHAPTER 4

Carol

April 1975

How, then, does one go about starting a financial institution for women?

From her position as cohost of the meeting, the first to gather a cross section of Denverites who'd gathered to brainstorm the very question on her mind, Carol B. Green felt somewhat ready to find an answer. For weeks now, she had filled up the lines in her notepad with the specifics—tidbits and details she had gleaned during the many meetings where she'd sat across the table from mostly men and asked them that same question.

As her knowledge expanded, her checklist grew long. Thus far, it included things like

- establish if you want a state or a national charter;
- apply for the charter;
- demonstrate the need for a financial entity such as a women's bank or credit union;
- conduct research and a feasibility study to help demonstrate specific community need;
- find a space to open up in, and renovate it if needed;

- set up a board;
- find eligible, qualified staff to run the bank.

But one sticking point had been emphasized at every meeting, whether it was during lunch in a downtown restaurant or over a cup of coffee in a corner office: Denver's banks were run, operated, owned, and overseen by the town's proverbial boy's club. And if that didn't demonstrate a need right there, what would?

She was no stranger to this boy's club overtone, and it wouldn't hold her back. Carol was now a successful local entrepreneur with many seasons running a business of her own in Denver. Part of her work included sitting in many meetings where, save for the secretary on hand to take notes, she was one of the few women, or sometimes the only woman, in the room. During those meetings, she observed how the balance of power often tipped away from her and toward a man, any man, in the room. She couldn't keep letting this happen.

As an owner of and the driving force behind her business, *her* name and reputation were on the line; she was quick to explain that she and her husband, Jules, had built a Weight Watchers empire together in the region, but it was with her sitting at the helm. But even then, men deferred to men. Men often appeared more comfortable doing business with each other. So, Carol B. Green found other tools to use. She became the woman who spoke up frequently to get things back on track and, more importantly, to get the answers she wanted. Men, she'd learned, expected a woman at their table to shyly say, "Well, I think . . . ," a hesitancy that never got very many women where they wanted to go.

And Carol B. Green—she was a woman who was going places.

It had been more than twenty years since LaRae Orullian had arrived in Denver, and seven years since that warm June day when a plane took Carol from Delaware to Denver's Stapleton Airport. She'd flown out ahead of Jules with their children to set things up. She and Jules, whom she had met in New York, had decided on Denver as the place to launch their first Weight Watchers franchise location. With the exception of postcards she'd gotten as a child from her grandmother Rose detailing how beautiful Colorado was, Carol knew very little about their new home. Her first sip of that crisp, distinct Colorado air was on moving day, the same day her plane landed.

During those early months, there was excitement about this new life and what it might bring. With the altitude-induced giddiness found only in places like Denver setting in, they'd built their business, establishing several successful Weight Watchers franchises. Like many young families, they quickly outgrew the cramped apartment they had rented across from the leafy shade of City Park. As the franchises expanded, the Greens moved around some, seeking a yard and more space, of course, but also a place that represented their success—a dream home, one they eventually found in the growing, posh suburb Cherry Hills.

Suburbs often are described as becoming mainstream in the post–World War II landscape, but older forebears can be found in many communities, and Denver was no exception. As the Colorado prairie began to evolve into real estate developments in the 1920s, planned outskirts-based communities grew. At that time, some developments adopted policies that served as barriers to entry. Take, for example, an advertisement for Wellshire Park, a planned community in Cherry Hills. The area started as over five hundred acres of Colorado prairie, but when it was ready for applicants, minorities were officially forbidden from buying homes in the neighborhood.

"The restrictions also provide that no property will ever be sold to Negroes, Chinese, Japanese or Mexicans" proclaimed a *Denver Post* article dated October 18, 1922.

Of the desired demographic, the article concludes, "such people seek homes where family tradition may be established and maintained, and where their children may be reared in an environment of stability, culture, and beauty."

South Hudson Parkway is a street in one such Denver suburb. The road itself divides at East Oxford, before joining into one winding boulevard that ends at a street called Quincy. There are fewer than twenty-five homes on this leafy street, most of which were originally built over a twenty-five-year period beginning in the 1950s and stretching into the mid-1970s. Although the construction style during this era is known as midcentury modern today, it was referred to as "contemporary" when it first hit the architecture world. And at the time of its construction, one of the most contemporary homes in Denver's suburbs was 4207 South Hudson Parkway.

It is often the natural bent of humanity to strive to outdo, and 4207 was one of several homes in the area built around the same time with that exact bent in mind. Constructed in 1964, 4207 was four thousand square feet of living space all contained on the same floor, located on a one-acre lot. Its moss rock (a Rocky Mountain staple pulled from the mines and beloved for its earthy, brown tones) and walnut exterior contained a structure with east and west wings, formal living and dining rooms, a carpeted den, a mosaic-tiled pool, and a sauna. Few homes in the region featured such amenities, but 4207 did.

"Distinctive and desirable," "expensive and expansive," "elegant," "exciting" wrote the undoubtedly motivated realtors listing the property in 1964 and again in 1966. In April 1971, 4207 hit the market once more, and despite the newer, equally impressive neighboring houses, the home continued to stand out. When Carol and Jules Green drove their shiny red family car up the circle drive and laid eyes on 4207, they knew it was the perfect place for their family not only to put down roots but also to celebrate their success. It was proof positive they'd done well together.

The Greens had met as teenagers working at a summer camp in upstate New York. Carol, then a high schooler from Queens, had taken a job as a counselor, while Jules, also a high schooler, who'd come with his family to the States from Argentina, worked as a waiter in the dining hall. When they met, Carol considered herself to be a very "fat, unattractive" young woman, but her weight issues were somewhat atypical. The culprit turned out to be a bad reaction to an operation when she was younger. When she was six, she'd gone into the hospital for a routine tonsillectomy, and her body had reacted abnormally to it. In a short span of time, she gained an alarming amount of weight, and while a steady series of diet pills sometimes helped, they also made her feel unsteady. Resolved that this was her life and she had to choose between letting diet pills rule her mind or feeling in control while being over-weight, Carol decided to stop the pills. She leaned on her academics and smarts, preferring to get lost in books over trifles like romance. When Jules showed an interest in her that summer, they first became camp friends.

She joined Weight Watchers after marrying Jules and having their first two children. Weight Watchers was started in Queens, but by the time Carol became a member, she, Jules, and their small family had moved to Delaware. She was impressed by how well the program worked for her. Eventually, Carol became an unrecognizable version of her former self. She lost forty pounds, trading her loose, shapeless garments for items that flattered her figure better. She now loved things in her closet like the lime-green shirtdress with a tie belt because it accented her newly defined waist.

Losing weight is one challenge, but as anyone who has taken a similar journey knows, the next step is of equal importance—that is, keeping the lost weight off. Carol kept it off. In place of the shy, pudgy bookworm was a woman who had gained more confidence than she'd ever imagined possible. This confidence would come in handy when she found herself sitting across from the men running banks in Denver, with a pepper shaker's worth of questions she needed answered.

It was that confidence (along with encouragement from Jules) that led her to enroll their children in day care so she could attend college classes. That same confidence brought her to podiums for speaking engagements, where she'd share her story of someone who'd taken con-trol of her life by changing her relationship with her body and with food. That same confidence was also present the day the franchise in Delaware approached her, asking if she might consider opening a Weight Watchers franchise together in Virginia.

She wasn't all that certain she wanted to be a partner, she'd recall, her brown eyes flashing brightly. But that didn't mean she wasn't interested in what a career with Weight Watchers might entail. When the franchise opportunity arose out west, she went back home to New York, where she attended trainings and was approved for the Colorado franchise. She and Jules paid the nominal $10,000 (about $88,200 in 2024 money) franchise fee and packed up. Initially, she and the two children had flown ahead to Colorado to get situated and let her set up business operations, while Jules stayed in Delaware to wrap things up. It was about a six-week adventure for both of them before Jules made the long westward drive across the prairies that once again united the family in Colorado.

Only time, hard work, and success had landed them the distinction of Mr. and Mrs. Green of 4207 South Hudson Parkway, where the walnut-paneled formal living room was now beginning to fill with meeting attendees. These folks were here to learn what Carol had discovered about starting a financial institution for women from scratch, with women in the leadership positions.

Word of this new, exciting project had spread among some of the business and social circles that Carol and her meeting cohost, Bonnie Andrikopoulos, ran in. Thus far, the meeting attendees were mostly women, dressed like the successes they were: Long skirts that fell to the calf, with matching blazers. Shimmery blouses underneath. Polka dots. The occasional striped or plaid number. Carefully manicured nails and casually made-up faces with eyeliner, a touch of blue eye shadow, or maybe peach blush. And pantyhose. Always fresh from the plastic eggs they sometimes came in and as non-baggy as possible, never runny, and as itchy and uncomfortable to wear as ever.

The few men in attendance had also dressed for the occasion in casual sport coats and slacks and shiny-toed shoes. Nobody in the room who sipped the soft drinks that Carol Green had offered to them could deny that 4207 was an impressive space. So impressive that the Green children, who now numbered three after Carol gave birth to a son in the middle of growing the business, not to mention the family dog, Cindy, were presumably somewhere in the house—maybe the den?—but nobody could hear them, and they certainly weren't underfoot.

It was a gorgeous home, but to Carol Green, 4207 South Hudson Parkway, despite its modern newness, status, spaciousness, and amenities, was a daily painful reminder. Her success in business could only take her so far because she was still a woman. Eventually, if she called on a bank for some help or some kind of services, the bank would probably ask after her husband. They would also prefer to speak with him over her.

Her home was a reminder of the day she learned that to the bank issuing its sizable mortgage, she was financially invisible.

A nonentity.

When the time had come for Carol and Jules to apply for a mortgage, the banker sitting across from them had been so blunt.

"We cannot count Carol's income," he had said. Consideration solely of Jules's income had put them in the position of having a lower income to report. In turn, this lower total income came with two risks. First, it could pave the way for a lower total mortgage loan and therefore less money and potentially less house. And it also meant the lender could grant them a less favorable interest rate.

Curious as to why Carol's income wouldn't be included, the Greens learned that because she was considered by the bank to be of childbearing age, Carol was categorized as someone who could be possibly pregnant at any given time. The implication was that pregnancy would derail her career. Her bank presumed that like most women who had children at that time, she would leave the working world to raise her and Jules's children, which would deflate their income.

"We already have children, and I still work outside the home," she explained. "I have a good income, and I run a successful, profitable business."

The bank's hands were tied. There was nothing anyone could personally do to help them out. This rule was part of the bank's policy.

At this exact same time across the nation, other excited couples no doubt faced bank loan officers. They shared their needs only to be met with the same disappointing and often surprising news: as far as the bank was concerned, they had only one income. Never mind the "possibly pregnant" clause and the invasive questions about birth control.

This prying was legally sanctioned and could be part of an interview that occurred before a couple found out whether they had received their loan. Banks didn't even have to provide a reason why the loan had been denied. Or, if you were Carol Green, you might learn that your income wouldn't count toward the mortgage.

That mortgage example right here at her fingertips presented one of many problems. Problems that she hoped could be properly solved once and for all by the people here in this room with her. It was time to start the meeting.

CHAPTER 5

The ERA

Spring 1975

With spring 1975 pressing onward, the first whispers of Denver's coming dry, hot summer began to hang in the air. Off in the distance, the Rocky Mountain peaks remained capped with white snow. In town and around the nation, progressive women like the members of Carol and Bonnie's group discovered an unlikely ally: the nation's newly appointed Republican president, Gerald R. Ford.

Ford occupied the Republican presidency during the unique, wobbly moment between Richard Nixon and Ronald Reagan, and before Democrat Jimmy Carter. Past and future Republicans might have skewed more toward encouraging women to seek out the roles of wife and mother, but Ford didn't shy away from supporting women's equality.

Through no fault of his own, Ford's ascent to the presidency occurred under unprecedented and bizarre circumstances. While Nixon was serving his second term in office, Ford was minding his own business as a long-standing member of Congress, where he represented Michigan's Fifth District. He was over twenty years into his career when the Watergate scandal erupted in the summer of 1972.

Further corruption plagued the administration. Nixon's vice president, Spiro Agnew, resigned in October 1973 after getting into hot water for alleged tax evasion that he insisted he hadn't done. Ultimately, Agnew was found guilty of the charges. Ford was then appointed by Nixon to replace Agnew as vice president. After Nixon formally announced his resignation some months later, Ford became the nation's thirty-eighth president.

Before the chaos of the Nixon administration had settled, Ford did two things that made many sit up and take note of him. The first was his pardon of Richard Nixon, citing the nation's need to heal.

The second was his support for the Equal Rights Amendment (ERA), which many of its backers hoped would represent ignition of a new revolution for women. In a photo taken to commemorate his support, Ford sits in the Oval Office wearing a light-colored suit jacket with a faint check pattern and a wide striped tie. Behind him stand a dozen well-dressed women, fashionable yet modest in their floral or pastel dresses or skirt suits. Among them are both Bella Abzug and Shirley Chisholm, two of the decade's most outspoken feminists and politicians from New York City.

For women, the air in the room was hopeful regarding the ERA that day for the first time in a while. The stack of documents on the table in front of Ford would declare his unwavering support for the ERA, a proposal that intended to end ongoing sexual discrimination against women.

The ERA was not new. A holdover from the prior wave of feminism, it had languished in Washington, DC, since 1923, when it had been introduced during a legislative session. The first-wave feminists of suffragettes had seen several wins, including getting women the right to vote. But the ERA was an entirely different matter. Fifty years had passed, and it was still stalled in the pipeline.

By 1972, the culture had begun to slowly transition away from the sleepy postwar 1950s stereotype of a housewife who relied solely on a husband to "take care of her." The notion of living happily ever after in a brand-new three-bedroom, two-and-a-half-bath suburban home (two story or ranch!) outfitted with brand-new appliances and china that wouldn't chip had continued to erode. Fewer women found complete fulfillment inside the home, where they'd once matched the curtains with chintz furnishings sure to impress the gals if they stopped by to play bridge or for a sip of coffee or something stronger.

Although not completely gone just yet, she still existed in plenty of places, even as she was continuing to undergo a metamorphosis. That same year, Title IX had passed, signaling a sea change in the nation's education systems. Title IX granted female students access to the same classes and activities, including sports, as their male counterparts. On the crest of this optimistic wave for women's rights, the ERA resurfaced and was formally reintroduced to Congress. It had cleared one hurdle by passing through Congress. Yet, despite all the enthusiasm at its reintroduction, the ERA was still stalled by 1974, when Ford sat at a table ready to sign on. It instead awaited ratification by enough states to make it an official constitutional amendment.

Amending anything in the US Constitution is a rightfully daunting undertaking. For a proposed amendment like the ERA to so much as move on to the states for a ratification vote, its language must pass Congress with a two-thirds vote by not just one but both houses. Congress can also call for a separate convention to focus on the proposed amendment.

After the ERA's congressional passage in March 1972, Colorado was one of the early states that voted to ratify. This reinforced Colorado's long-standing tradition as a more progressive friend to women and supporter of women's equality. The ERA's clock was ticking, since it came with a seven-year deadline: if thirty-eight states didn't vote to ratify within that time, by 1979, the amendment would be considered dead. Little did everyone posing for that photo with Ford know that fifty years later the ERA would still not be a part of the Constitution. To this day, it remains stalled because the required final three states to ratify did so after 1982, leaving the amendment yet to be considered valid.

CHAPTER 6

Betty

Fall 1975

The minute she learned there would be meetings about setting up a financial institution for women, Betty Sue Borwick Freedman couldn't wait to be there.

Attending a meeting like this was just one of many items on Betty's seemingly endless list of tasks, events, or gatherings. She was a college-educated woman who felt confined by the expected role of housewife, and one mission she held dear was contributing to Denver's future beyond the close-knit Jewish community where she'd grown up. Betty also strove to bridge communities within Denver. She always invited both her Jewish and non-Jewish friends to participate in her charitable activities. As a good-looking woman with natural charm, her social prowess had won her friendships with civic leaders, bankers, oil men, businesspeople, and artisans. Her connections ran a spectrum and helped bring a variety of people together to build patronage for local institutions, including the Denver Art Museum and Public Library.

As a native Denverite, her name and comings and goings had frequently appeared in the local society pages. Born in 1922 to Hattie and Benjamin Borwick, she was the youngest of five siblings who spanned twenty-one years. She grew up in a modest duplex near City Park, in a close-knit pioneering Jewish family. Her maternal forebears had emigrated from czarist pogroms and then, in 1882, helped to establish a Hebrew agriculture colony in Cotopaxi, Colorado. But growing up, Betty had badly wanted to venture out of east Denver and into the world that lay beyond the Rocky Mountains. In her mind, Denver had always seemed small compared to other places where she'd traveled or lived. She often somewhat affectionately referred to it as "Cow Town," as though it might be more of an outpost in a spaghetti western than a sleek, sought-after cosmopolitan metropolis.

After devouring the works of Dorothy Parker and F. Scott Fitzgerald, a young, bookish Betty Sue dreamed of one day becoming a writer and going to New York City, where she'd splash in the fountain at the Plaza Hotel. She even made her way out of Denver, but her journey out and up wasn't always an easy or glamorous one.

Her father, Benjamin, had emigrated from Odessa, which was then part of Russia, at age sixteen. He was an enterprising young man who'd gotten his start selling umbrellas. Benjamin also worked hard to learn English, and in 1900, he founded the pioneering Colorado Electric Wiring Company.

On a grim February day, Benjamin suffered a massive heart attack. Hattie ran to find a doctor, and it was a terrified thirteen-year-old Betty who held him tight during the agonizing moments as he slipped away, eventually dying in her arms. His sudden death during the depths of the Great Depression left a widowed Hattie in less-than-desirable financial circumstances, but Benjamin had provided a college insurance policy that eventually paid Betty's tuition at Baltimore's Goucher College. Some twenty years before, when Betty's eldest brother, David, was college aged, Hattie and Benjamin had disagreed about paying his tuition to attend university out of state. Hattie took it upon herself to deliver the boy to Stanford Law School. She was unable to write the check for David's tuition because at that time, like most married women of that era, Hattie couldn't have a checking account in her own name. So Hattie forged a check and drove her son to California.

With David safely at college, she wrote a telegram back to Benjamin that family members recall read something like "honor the check or put me in jail!" Benjamin agreed to pay it.

Benjamin had left enough so that Betty was able to enroll in the college of her choosing in 1940. Before Betty started her courses at Goucher, her brother Charles set her up on a date with one of his fraternity brothers at the University of Pennsylvania. Marshall Freedman was a premed student and a bit of an egghead who helped keep the fraternity's grade point average afloat. Betty and Marshall dated throughout college. After Pearl Harbor, Marshall enrolled in Penn's medical school in army uniform. Betty, who'd by then developed into a talented writer, gave Marshall an ultimatum: propose marriage or break up. Betty hadn't anticipated she'd get much pushback. She wanted very much to be his wife; she *loved* him. After he broke her heart, she returned to her room, gathered every one of the love letters he had ever written to her, and set them all ablaze.

After the split with Marshall, Betty reconnected with a previous beau, the handsome Bob Shapiro, who'd gone to Stanford and then enlisted in the navy's officer-training program. Their marriage was happy but short lived. After their honeymoon, Bob shipped off to the Pacific war. Betty moved into his parents' home in Hollywood, California, where she got to work writing radio plays. When the war ended, Bob had been scheduled to return to LA just in time to sit in the audience as one of her plays was read on a CBS radio broadcast. He never made it back. The day before the play was to go live, a telegram arrived informing Mrs. Shapiro that Bob had died after contracting polio while swimming in a pool at an army officers' club in Manila. A devastated Betty could hardly listen to the broadcast of her handiwork.

Meanwhile, in the time since breaking off their relationship, Marshall had undergone some changes of his own. When a mutual friend shared Betty's latest news, his heart leapt. Finally, he had come to his senses about Betty.

He was now an MD, and when he arrived on her in-laws' doorstep, proposing then and there, she had replied, "Marshall, there's nothing sadder than a dead love."

But he wasn't deterred. For months, he persisted and eventually prevailed. They eloped to Tijuana and then were married by a rabbi at her sister's home in Denver. After spending time in Alabama, where he was stationed in the army, and Los Angeles, they moved on to Minnesota when Marshall took a job at the Mayo Clinic. Despite Betty's devastating loss, they felt lucky to be together, and welcomed their firstborn, a boy they named Jonathan and called "Jon." The Freedmans made friends easily with the fellows at the clinic and attended art shows and cocktail parties with them.

But just as Los Angeles had, Minnesota would eventually become a place of ghosts for Betty. Dougie, a cheerful, beautiful baby, was born a year after Jon. Although she wasn't a doctor, Betty had a mother's intuition about Dougie that engaged early on, because he wasn't developing like Jon had. She couldn't help but worry when Dougie, compared to Jon and other babies, didn't reach the milestone of sitting up as expected. Dougie also suffered from terrible stomach cramps. Eventually, she took him to Mayo for a more thorough examination.

A famous pediatrician looked him over and eventually tried to reassure a worried Betty. "Mrs. Freedman, don't worry your pretty little head," he had said. "Some babies are just slower."

But her "pretty little head" had been correct to worry about Dougie. By the time he was six months old, he still couldn't sit up and spent his days screaming in pain and frustration. Feeling ever more helpless by the day and longing for a way to bring their baby some relief—any relief—a desperate Marshall got to work. He dug into his textbook and discovered the rare genetic disorder Tay-Sachs disease.

Tay-Sachs impacts a disproportionate number of Ashkenazic Jews, but it is also found in children in the overall Jewish population. It is caused by a missing enzyme that helps to break down fatty substances called gangliosides. If gangliosides build up, they become toxic in the brain and then affect the function of a child's nerve cells. As the disease progresses, its victims lose control over their muscles, which leads to blindness and paralysis and, ultimately, to death.

Although it's difficult to identify outright, Tay-Sachs can sometimes still be easily ruled out. One way to determine whether it is present is to look for a cherry-red spot in the child's eye. Strapping on his doctor's headlamp, Marshall peered into his tiny son's beautiful eyes, known in the family as "the Borwick eyes," and spotted his death knell. Dougie had Tay-Sachs. He wouldn't ever throw a baseball. He and Jon would not grow up to be scheming brothers like Wally and Beaver on *Leave It to Beaver* because Dougie was not going to survive this. Both boys were so young, especially Dougie, but Betty and Marshall had no other choice but to look on as Dougie's deterioration progressed. They held him in their arms, hearts, and minds as symptoms took hold, replacing milestones. Eventually, when Dougie could no longer metabolize food, he slowly went deaf and then blind. In the middle of a frigid Minnesota February, Dougie took his final breath, and like Betty's father had done all those years ago, and Bob had done far away in Manila, Dougie slipped away.

After they laid him to rest, a gray slowly crept into the corners of their life, spilling into the center, where it threatened to level them all in its wake.

Marshall was destroyed by his inability to help his ailing son. He had once chosen medicine over love, reconciled with his sweetheart, and gotten that rare second chance with her, and yet, through his small son, he had uncovered a limitation no doctor or parent should have to. Devastated, he developed an allergic reaction to the mandatory rubber gloves doctors used during surgery. In an attempt to save his career, he switched teams, going from surgeon to internist, when he was dealt yet another blow: Mayo would not offer him a permanent job. Meanwhile, an equally destroyed and heartbroken Betty fell into a state of depression. She would be found staring off into the cruelty of the Minnesota winter that had chewed her up and swallowed her whole that year. Her baby, her youngest, her little son was gone. Dougie's absence, and the silence that came with it, festered in the air of their home.

With Dougie gone and Marshall now facing less-than-promising career prospects, they had no desire to stay on and take their chances in cold, flat Minnesota. Marshall and Betty agreed that what the family probably needed most of all was a fresh start. As the weather thawed, they concluded that it was time for their little family to return to Betty's mountain roots. Denver would become their next home, and with Borwick family connections in the community, the fresh start would have a little help.

And so, in 1954, after a long hiatus, Betty found herself right smack dab back in Cow Town. She hadn't exactly become the East Coast Dorothy Parker or Zelda Fitzgerald type that she'd hoped, but she now had an active boy to raise and ideas for children's books to write.

Three years later, Betty was pregnant again, and fate stared her in the face. Statistically, one of four babies born to two carriers of the Tay-Sachs gene could have the fatal disease, which could happen randomly. With no ability to test for it, they would be flying blind, but decided to take their chances. After nine nerve-wracking months, Betty gave birth to Tracy, their healthy daughter. She could never replace Dougie, but Tracy was part of their fresh start. Early on, to their relief, they found that Tracy, whom they'd nicknamed "Sparkle," didn't have cherry-red spots when they flashed the light into her eyes.

With Jon and Tracy growing and healthy, the next thing on the agenda for Dr. and Mrs. Marshall Freedman was to make names for themselves in Denver's community. Marshall, who had struggled to open a private practice, eventually became a pioneering gastroenterologist, which required him to be on call many nights. Betty resented his nonstop work and absence at night, when he'd return home with just enough time to change clothes, grab a fast breakfast, and fly out the door to make an 8:00 a.m. hospital round. She developed outside interests and social connections while attending hospital dinners or fundraisers. Like in Minnesota, as a couple, Marshall and Betty were popular with their new circle of friends, which helped when it came time to hold charity auctions and fashion shows or to fundraise for the civic works she eventually put her stamp on. Despite a life of loss and pain, Betty was a classy woman who surrounded herself with beauty, which she prized and craved; it inspired her. Since she couldn't have the excitement, glamour, and culture she'd soaked up living on both coasts, she instead worked tirelessly to bring them out west. In her efforts to make the place more palatable to her tastes, she also found her people.

As their children were growing up and out, *the* place to be on weekend nights, for those in the know, was the Freedman home. Their 1958 ranch-style house with its circle drive was proof positive that appearances can be deceiving. What guests found once they walked up that drive and into the nondescript home was the real draw.

Those in attendance at one of their famous gatherings never knew exactly what or whom to expect. But they could anticipate an unforgettable, fun time. One week, a guest might find themselves chatting with artist Helen Redman, who had painted portraits of Betty in a crimson sheath dress made of Thai silk and of Marshall performing a gastroscopy on a patient. Another time, maybe it would be a lecturer, novelist, orchestra conductor, or journalist or Marshall's gastroenterology fellows, a handful of local socialites, and kindred spirits from one of the many committees to which Betty tirelessly devoted her time and energy. Whoever was in attendance could expect delicious food and drink and lively conversation with a revolving cast of characters. All of this took place surrounded by the multitude of intriguing works of art that the Freedmans had collected over time and kept on display in their home.

In addition to her smarts, Betty had always been a looker and a sharp dresser. Some might have considered bits of her wardrobe to be on the flashy side, but she took a great deal of pride in her appearance. She often wore a signature red lipstick and styled her hair to complement her gorgeous, large, blue Borwick eyes. Her closet was full of wonderful pieces—bright A-line spaghetti-strap numbers, silk Pucci prints, mink, shiny costume jewelry—items that shared the story of a worldly, successful doctor's wife.

It was Betty's turn to spread her wings and fly a little. No doubt she had been equally choosy when it was time to put on her outfit for the meeting at Carol Green's home. What exactly did one wear to such a meeting? She'd heard about the "Weight Watchers lady" and her bank idea somewhere and found it to be a keen one. A financial institution for women by women in Cow Town?

Betty couldn't sign up fast enough.

CHAPTER 7

Well, Women, of Course

By car, Carol Green's home was about twenty minutes south of Betty's, giving Betty just enough time to think things over a little bit on the ride there. Once she arrived, she greeted Carol and her cohost, Bonnie, and joined the group. It seemed that everyone there, whether a newcomer or a returning guest, was just as curious and excited about the idea as she was.

Like many women of her generation, Betty might not have been overly involved in her own family's financial matters, but as an avid fundraiser, she knew how to help raise a heap of money within a specified time frame. She also knew how to get people to gather to accomplish common goals.

When addressing the room, Carol and Bonnie, the entrepreneur and the activist, must have made a somewhat curious picture to the onlookers. They shared a mission, yet they couldn't have seemed more different. If Carol was known for her business acumen, Bonnie was equally known for her involvement in the local feminist movement. She was a divorcée who had moved to Denver from Wyoming to attend nursing school, making a name for herself through her work with the local chapter of the National Organization for Women (NOW). Bonnie would also coauthor a book about abortion and was highly vocal about women's rights.

When Carol spoke, she began by telling the group about what had inspired her to explore the idea of starting up a women's bank.

That prior winter, she'd been laid up in the hospital recovering from a staph infection she'd contracted during a routine procedure. Stuck in her hospital room with time on her hands and life literally going on without her outside her window, she could only read and sleep so much. Eventually, she'd had no choice but to befriend the television in her room. As game shows, news programs, and soap operas droned on, the idle time was anything but relaxing for her. Carol was an independent woman. She'd grown up watching as her father put her mother down, even discouraging her from learning to drive, and vowed her life wouldn't mirror that of her mother's. Besides, time was money, or some kid-related activity, or maybe even dinner with Jules. Then something on the TV caught her eye. Something wonderful.

"One program on the television was about the group of women in New York City who were about to open up a women's bank," she recalled. And watching the program got her thinking a great deal.

Denver, she hoped, was about to become part of a vibrant sisterhood, because women's banks were not new. They were actually making a comeback. The first prominent women's bank opened in Clarksville, Tennessee, in October 1919. A Mrs. F. J. Runyon served as president.

Named the First Woman's Bank of Tennessee, the bank was capitalized at $15,000 after 150 shares of the bank's stock were sold at $100 each. Rules specified that no one was allowed to buy more than two of the bank's shares, which sold out within a day. The date the bank opened, customer deposits into the bank surpassed $20,000.

The bank remained profitable through 1925, and in 1926, it merged into the First Trust and Savings Bank. At the time, representatives cited a bad fall taken by Mrs. F. J. Runyon as the reason for the merger, but records also reflect that the bank had begun to experience some financial hardship at that time. An article in the *Clarksville Leaf-Chronicle* summarized the merger:

> Since the day it opened for business, the First Woman's Bank has enjoyed a growth that has been more than gratifying to its officers and stockholders. Organized in October 1919, the bank became at once an important factor in the business circles of this and the surrounding counties. Under the capable management of Mrs. F. J. Runyon as president, and Mrs. Matt G. Lyle as cashier, together with the board of directors consisting entirely of women, the bank, being the first or one of the first to be entirely under the management of women, has attracted wide attention over the United States and even in some foreign countries.

"The idea of such an institution resonated with me," she continued. Carol wasn't alone in her thinking. The idea resonated with Bonnie Andrikopoulos too, and from there, the idea grew. To most who vowed to take it seriously, a financial institution for women seemed marvelous, really.

From her hospital room, Carol started what became a lot of research after that TV program. Eventually, she'd even gotten so bold as to phone the women at the New York City bank, where the impressive Madeline McWhinney, a native Denverite herself, was the woman bank executive who had been lined up to run the institution called First Women's Bank.

"I phoned to ask what the target demographic was," Carol told the group. "They said, 'Well, women, of course.'"

Well, women, of course.

It made logical sense, but would a bank like this limit or deter potential customers who presumed the bank wasn't for them?

The conversation in Carol's living room then turned to the ultimate question: How could they set up a place like the one in New York out here in Denver? Luckily for the group, Carol had already covered a lot of ground on that front. As they went over the list of needed tasks, two items in the bunch stood out to Betty: set up a board and hire qualified staff to run the entity.

A women's bank would inevitably need eligible women to run it.

Finding a qualified woman in Denver to run such a bank might prove to be difficult. There weren't very many women in higher-up positions at the banks. Not here, and not elsewhere in the country for that matter.

Part of Carol's initial inquiry had included just checking to see if a woman *could* serve as a bank president. Her curiosity extended to wondering if there were any women running banks and what was the current highest position a woman held in a bank. Did the men running the financial show in town think it was even possible? Could a woman—possibly her, even—run a bank? She'd first tested her theory out on her own banker (a man, of course).

He had been blunt. "Carol, I think you can do anything," he'd said. His words were semi-reassuring, but saying "you can do anything" was one thing. Doing the "anything" would be an entirely different undertaking.

As Betty listened to the meeting, she felt the familiar tingle of excitement at the beginning of a project. These women might not know it yet, but they needed her. Not only for her willingness to work on projects, but for her Rolodex of contacts. She knew the who's who in town. Surely in the course of their work, there would be a need for somebody she could point them toward, and when that moment came, she'd be more than happy to share.

It didn't take long.

In those early days, one article in particular had circulated among the group. It excited almost everyone as the attendees passed around the rustling photocopies from a February 1975 issue of *Colorado Business Magazine*. It was the article on the bottom half of the page that piqued their interest.

Someone in the room read aloud as everyone else read along silently. "'New Hands at the Till: Women in Banking'" began the reader.

The article contained fresh data and related directly to their project. According to it, four women currently had the position of vice president or higher at nearby Colorado banks. Of that four, only one woman had attained her position by working her way up within the industry. The others had, in essence, inherited their roles due to nepotism or directly through the death of male relatives. Being able to actually run a bank and knowing what it took to do so was an important distinction. One woman, it seemed, had extensive knowledge of both. Her name was LaRae Orullian.

"Does anybody know LaRae Orullian?"

When LaRae's name appeared in the article and came up in conversation, Betty nodded excitedly. She knew this woman well.

Of course, she'd seen her at the bank. Guaranty was founded by the local Jewish community, which had included several of Betty's relatives. As such, her family had some accounts there. She also knew LaRae socially, seeing her out and about at various events and fundraisers. Beyond knowing and respecting LaRae, Betty also genuinely liked her. She'd be perfect for this project. Betty just knew it. She wasn't afraid to voice her conviction about LaRae Orullian then and there.

"I do," said Betty.

CHAPTER 8

The Nuts and Bolts of It All

December 1975

In what felt like no time at all, eight months had passed since that first meeting in Carol Green's spacious home in Cherry Hills Village. By the time December 1975 rolled around, the group had grown so much bigger that they moved meetings to the Weight Watchers meeting room in her office, located about three miles away. In addition to Carol, Bonnie, and Betty, they were joined by several core members that included Barbara Sudler, another socialite and fundraiser; Wendy Davis, a local attorney and councilwoman; Edna Mosley, an advocate with the local chapter of the National Association for the Advancement of Colored People (NAACP); and Beverly Martinez-Grall, who worked at the local CBS affiliate, channel 2, and had her own program. Mike Feinstein, Carol's accountant, was also a long-standing attendee, as were several other men. Rounding out the group was a revolving cast of interested and curious Denverites.

The room where the group sat on this particular evening had hosted plenty of stories. Typically, they included the many triumphs and tribulations of those looking to reduce their weight and increase their confidence. Carol Green had even shared the story of her own weight-loss journey within these walls. This Thursday evening, it hosted a different sort of group on a different sort of mission.

By the time the meeting began at 7:30 p.m., the sun had already been down behind the Rockies for nearly three hours. People remarked about how it was getting colder and darker out as they headed toward the holidays and the shortest day of the year. Despite it being the end of the workday for those who worked traditional business hours outside their homes and despite the lengthening darkness, the air inside the room was often electric. Attendees talked among themselves, settling in, preparing to take notes, or discussing holiday plans or the latest news or the weather, until Carol Green called the meeting to order at 7:47.

As was the custom by now, Carol headed up the meetings and often spoke first. She had made inroads with Madeline McWhinney of New York City's First Women's Bank, which had opened about six weeks prior. The big news was that McWhinney had agreed to help the group over the phone from time to time.

Compared to New York City, where a handful of qualified, skilled women could take the helm at First Women's Bank, things were a bit sparse out west. Colorado still boasted few women currently sitting on bank boards, and no women were serving in the role of bank president.

However, "A number of women have moved into significant positions such as vice president," Carol said, addressing the group. "But when we looked at the numbers from a percentage standpoint, it can be seen that the percentage is very small. One of our goals is [to] fill any position in a bank with qualified women."

Looking out at the group assembled before her, Carol smiled. "What do you believe some of our long- and short-term goals should be? Although many specific goals will come out of the feasibility study, we need to establish certain philosophical directions."

Feasibility had been on their minds since Carol had first mentioned it as part of the checklist. A feasibility study wouldn't come cheap, not then and not now. They are conducted to ascertain whether or not an idea will work. They also require careful selection of a team to conduct the study properly; it also must be completed within a strict timeline. In the case of the Women's Bank, the feasibility study would be their first real indication of public interest in a women's bank. While it was not a guarantee of success, it would reveal if there was interest in banking downtown or at a bank that might have the word "women" in its name. (Might? The name of the proposed bank would be the subject of much lively debate.)

To conduct a feasibility study, members of the group ultimately agreed to the following terms:

1.   Each member would give $1,000 of their own money (roughly $6,700 in 2024 money).
2.   They could then use those funds to hire an outside party to conduct the study.

The study would be their first concrete step in working toward founding the bank. It also would be the first hurdle. If the study suggested the project was too infeasible, well, that would be that. And now that everyone had put in the not-insignificant sum of $1,000, they all had skin in the game. The feasibility study would give them important data, like what other banks already operated within range and what they provided customers or what banking needs might lie outside the proposed location. They hoped the results would tell them definitively whether the bank should be downtown or if they should look elsewhere for a location.

Marianne Krauss, one attendee, was the first to answer Carol's question about philosophy. "Firstly, I feel certain that what everyone wants is a bank that will be a successful business venture. This, to me, is the most important issue." There were many murmurs of agreement.

Carol nodded. "This is a goal that's been prevalent since our very first meeting—that is, that women can set up a very successful institution."

Setting up a successful institution would become a pesky issue pertaining to the bank's founding, though. A successful bank requires candidates who are considered ideal. This meant that while taking a chance on women and the underbanked populous, they still needed viable, creditworthy clients, or, at least to have clients on their way to viability and creditworthiness.

Overhead, lights hummed and a steady stream of blue cigarette smoke curled, mingling with the scents of women's perfume and men's cologne.

"What's the time frame for getting organized?" asked Wendy Davis, an attorney, looking up from her notes.

By now, anyone who had attended one or more of these meetings knew there were a lot of moving parts for the group to consider. They wanted to appeal to a wide audience, which meant conducting outreach to as many people as possible. They also wanted to find the best people to run and advise the bank. Committees (marketing, stock subscription, planning) would be formed out of the most interested members and those best qualified to assist. Much of their protocol would be learned and adjusted in real time. Committee members would join together to help complete those tasks that now went far beyond the key points Carol Green had first jotted down during her informational meetings with executives that past spring. With so much to do, they decided the best plan involved choosing what logistics could be tackled early on and then figuring out what committees could take on other tasks. They would need a building, for instance, but once they had the results of the feasibility study, they could form a subcommittee to start looking in the right area and bring some options back to the larger group.

One woman participant who had been very generous with her knowledge but who was absent this evening was Dr. Doris Drury.

Dr. Drury worked as an economics professor at the University of Denver. Among her many accolades, she was appointed to the Commission on the Status of Women by Colorado governor John Arthur Love in 1973. Knowledgeable, brilliant, and generous with her time, Dr. Drury was often called on to consult on this economic idea or to speak to her expertise on that economics panel. She was also known as an outspoken advocate for marginalized groups.

She'd come to any group, including this one, and with eyes twinkling and in the remnants of her Kentucky drawl, she'd share her invaluable insight. In the case of one of the group's most critical and much discussed missing links, the feasibility study, she'd offered plenty of advice. This evening, location was on Dr. Drury's mind even though she couldn't be present.

"Dr. Drury is ill and couldn't be here tonight, but she wanted me to tell you that when we do the study, we need to include the south side of town too," Carol said.

The bank's physical place was just one of the many decisions that would rely on the results of the group's feasibility study. They were still looking for the right entity to conduct the study, but in the interim, sorting out what to ask when it was time for the study was still progress.

In addition to providing insight into how feasible a bank would be for a particular community and at a proposed location, the study would also tell the committee how feasible *any* new bank would be, not specifically a women's bank.

Location is an important factor that can make or break any business, and banks aren't immune. While today it's easy to bank remotely or even using a smartphone and sometimes go months without ever setting foot into an actual bank, in 1975 nearly all banking had to be done in person. The old saying about real estate (location, location, location) was certainly true for banks before online banking. It didn't matter how wonderful or potentially profitable a bank was; if it wasn't conveniently located, it would be more likely to fail. There were also local and state laws to consider during setup. And in Denver, a law on the books in 1975 prohibited what is known as branch banking.

Branch banks are standard now. When you open an account with an accredited bank, you can use any of its branches or automated teller machines (ATMs) across the country. This convenience is taken for granted but wasn't the case in Denver in 1975. Nationwide, ATMs were newfangled machines that only existed in their infancy. Denver's lack of branch banks meant that when it was time to choose where to do their banking, consumers were essentially choosing just one location. Often, there was a specific reason that a consumer sought out a bank, and it was usually because the bank was close to home or where they worked. The group hoped the feasibility study would demonstrate both the local need for and a customer base interested in specifically banking at their bank within the Denver metro area.

From his spot in the audience, Frank Vick, another attorney, piped up: "Feasibility research usually comes in two stages. I recommend at least an initial look to see if this project is warranted."

According to Carol's research, getting preliminary results from a feasibility study took roughly a month. Under that sample timeline, a study conducted in early December could provide results in January. "That means in January, we can file for a charter," she said. "We also have to decide if we want this bank to be a state or nationally chartered one."

A state or national charter would be a frequent discussion topic in the following weeks. It was right up there with who the customer would be and where they would be located. A bank's charter is a formal decree. It is also the license from the government granting it permission to perform banking activities. Its state or national designation signifies whether the state government or the federal government has granted the bank its permission to operate. National charters also come with an extra identifier that state charters don't contain—that of "NA" in the bank's title. The NA meant the group would take the extra steps necessary to attain the designation and that they were adhering to local, state, and federal laws. It would be an extra jewel in their crowns, if they could achieve it.

Charters also help dictate certain bank protocols and regulations around things like bank stock ownership. Ownership is a critical subject because it indicates influence. If an entity owns too much of the bank, that entity runs against regulations put into place to prevent this very thing from happening. Earlier that year, First Women's Bank in New York had opened with a state charter, which limited each of its investors to a maximum of 2.5 percent of the bank's total stock subscription. Perhaps because of this, some speculated, it had struggled to find enough investors.

Proposed locations were another hot topic on which everyone had an opinion. For some, downtown was an ideal spot to open a bank like this. Women were returning to work or choosing full-time work outside the home in droves, many in offices located downtown. Downtown had also begun to shed some of the run-down identity associated with Jack Kerouac's *On the Road*, with flophouses and urban blight giving way instead to restored historical landmarks joining shiny, modern highrises and open squares. At lunchtime or on weekends, pedestrians and passersby could now take in live music or soak up the sunshine.

Whom the bank project ultimately intended to serve was another topic that took up a great deal of conversation. Would it aim to solely serve the underbanked and marginalized communities like women, or would it serve everyone with an interest in doing business there? At one point in the evening, Bob Joselyn, who'd been part of the group long enough to share his convictions, was compelled to challenge aloud the premise that the bank's market should just be women.

"If the market is limited to just women, the bank is in big trouble," he said.

As some heads swiveled in his direction and a handful of attendees wondered why he would say something that damning to a roomful of people having a meeting about setting up a women's bank, Bob clarified. "Women alone don't represent a viable enough market for any single bank," he said. "This might even be an image mistake."

Bob's words had piqued plenty of interest, but he also had a solution. This bank couldn't just be another run-of-the-mill entity like the dozens already found along Seventeenth Street. "This ought to be a people's bank," he said. "Objectives here should be to offer fair and equal treatment to all groups."

The room stilled and Bonnie Andrikopoulos nodded. "I agree, Bob. It describes downtown people like women and minorities, and the suburbs don't really fit with those groups, in my mind."

Susanne Bailey, an early attendee who also sometimes kept the minutes, had been relatively quiet for most of the meeting. With so much yet unknown and so many opinions in the room, some sparring among members was expected. Tonight's meeting wasn't even halfway through, but it was time for her to speak up and add her thoughts to the mix.

"This bank needs to look for two other types of people besides women and minorities," she said.

The first, in her mind, were people whom she loosely described as "enlightened, solid financial giants." The second consisted of "young entrepreneurs with good ideas and who needed financing."

To Dave Jennings, everything boiled down to demographics. Research would help here: "Who isn't being served—who isn't being reached—are the questions. Not whether the bank should be uptown or downtown."

The name and location were debated a bit more that night. There was more to discuss, however, and the meeting continued. By the time it ended and Betty reached for her coat, she wondered if Marshall might be home yet. He would get a kick out of some of these folks. And maybe there would be time for them to have a discussion about the meeting before heading off to bed.

CHAPTER 9

Edna

How does an institution ensure it properly represents and reflects the community it serves?

As one of several women of color in the group, Edna Mosley had attended meetings for a while now. Like several other longer-term members in attendance, she had first come at the invitation of Bonnie Andrikopoulos, liked the idea, and ended up staying.

Similar to Betty Freedman, Edna had children who were now mostly grown and out of the house, so she had the kind of time one needed to be able to pour herself into her work and her activism. She'd already made a name for herself as a member of the NAACP and an outspoken advocate on the town's affirmative action committee. Getting involved with a bank that aimed to serve marginalized, underbanked clients like women and minorities was a natural fit for her.

As meetings and time progressed, she'd grown accustomed to Carol Green leading the discussion and to her friend Bonnie assuming the position of coleader. Like other women in the group, she'd also even gotten used to the inclusion of a few men.

In December 1975, disco was making its move from the underground-club scene to the mainstream on pop radio, where it secured a grip on the *Billboard* Top 40 with glitzy girl trio Silver

Convention's "Fly, Robin, Fly" rooted at number one for the second week in a row. Just behind them at the number two slot was "That's the Way (I Like It)" by KC and the Sunshine Band. Christmas lights were starting to go up, a chill was in the air, and, in some places in Colorado, there was already a bit of crunchy snow on the ground.

On December 4, the meeting had started off predictably enough. Edna listened to the back-and-forth, noting down any new bits here or there that she'd not yet heard. She'd heard quite a lot by this point, to be honest.

"Part of my research has entailed finding out if a bank like the one we are exploring might be ruled prejudicial," Carol Green said. "I found that all signs pointed to that not being the case."

Initially, the group had viewed the bank as one that proclaimed equality, rather than a women-specific bank. To reinforce its nonprejudicial status, Carol said, "This bank would have a set of rules that would apply to all people."

Edna listened while Carol added that the bank likely wouldn't immediately be able to finance large projects like construction or big business launches. They'd start smaller and grow. "A more immediate goal would instead be to set up extensive educational initiatives," she said. The bank's financial planning center she envisioned would work with women, minorities, and others. "The objective would be to never forget the customer."

Never forget the customer.

When Dave Jennings mentioned the bank's demographics, Edna perked up. After all, the matter of whom the bank would serve was entirely its point. This was her time to speak.

"Accessibility is important," she said. "Inner-city people are less mobile. They need a bank more."

Bonnie nodded. "My feeling is that women and minorities have been discriminated against more. A bank could be successful by appealing to these segments of the population."

With the dozen-plus attendees passionately making their cases, it was easy to wonder if they could pull off something that also satisfied everyone's ideas. Still, Edna was an activist. Even the *idea* of a bank that would serve the marginalized might be ahead of its time, but it was still a long time coming. She was excited to be part of these meetings.

Edna wasn't the only minority woman advising and participating in the group. There was also Beverly Martinez-Grall, whom Edna already knew, and later, they would be joined by several others from different racial backgrounds. Being included in even this nitty-gritty stuff ensured that Denver's minority populations would have proper representation and a voice. Knowing that felt good.

In Edna, the group had themselves a real Wild West "outlaw" of sorts. What few people who encountered the well-dressed, elegant pilot's wife, who'd once posed together with him and their children for the cover of *Jet* magazine, knew was that she also was a self-professed fugitive of sorts.

I paid for my ticket. I'm not moving.

The year was 1954, the same one when LaRae Orullian moved to Denver. Edna Mosley was twenty-nine and a wife and mother with small children. That summer, she took a train over one thousand miles from Denver to Helena, Arkansas, to visit family with some of her children in tow. Their visit had gone well enough, but she got into trouble on the platform while waiting on the train that would carry them back to Denver. She also ended up spending the night in the local jail.

Edna's resolute statement and the reason for her trouble on the day of her arrest might have surprised other onlookers on the train platform who didn't know her. But it would not shock anyone who did, especially her children. Her daughter, sometimes called "little Edna," grew up beyond accustomed to her parents' bold and sometimes eyebrow-raising positions on social issues. She remembers her parents, John and Edna, insisting they had every right to go where any other human being went, regardless of their race, origin, creed, religion, or otherwise. John and Edna didn't just talk the talk; they quite literally walked the walk. Sometimes, walking the walk meant bringing the kids along to the "white church" across town. Sometimes, to their chagrin, the children would find themselves dropped off by their parents to go on in.

We have as much right to worship the same God as the white folks do, they told the children. When John or Edna made friends, at a time when different races socializing wasn't common, they weren't afraid to diversify. The Mosleys entertained friends of different races in their home, and they also weren't afraid to elicit stares from onlookers with their blended friendships on full public display.

In 1954, it is impossible to say what it was about the three Mosleys that caught the strange white man's eyes on the platform that day in Helena. Something about them surely did. It could have been the children, dressed in their finest Sunday outfits, complete with starched collars and shiny shoes. Or maybe it was beautiful Edna herself. A slim woman with deep brown eyes and freshly pressed hair, she took a great deal of care in every aspect of her life and her appearance. She was a seamstress from a young age, and she and the children often wore clothes she had made that carried her very own bespoke label. On the platform that fateful day, she was a vision. A bright-yellow pop of color courtesy of her sundress and matching parasol. White gloves to clutch her black alligator handbag completed the outfit.

Whatever it was about them, as the fresh, smartly dressed trio waited for their train amid intercom announcements and the occasional chug and whistle of the trains, the strange white man approached them.

He demanded that they leave the train platform immediately. But Edna was firmly rooted on that platform. Just because racism was all around them here in Helena didn't mean she had to accept it quietly. Not from him. Not from anybody.

The South was one story, but moving out west still hadn't been a cure-all to escape the deep social and cultural racism she'd battled growing up. Segregation, oppression, and discrimination were also alive and well in Denver. For generations, the region was known as a home to pioneers, cowboys, and prospectors. But Denver has also quietly served as home to a robust, entrepreneurial, and pioneering African American community. And along with it, slow fights for more civil rights.

Some of its most famous African American residents have included James Beckwourth, a trapper, and trader Barney L. Ford, who built the Inter-Ocean Hotel, once the biggest hotel in the city. By 1881, Denver saw African American John T. Gunnel sit in the Colorado legislature. Hair-products legend Madam C. J. Walker called Denver home at one time. Meanwhile, Lewis Douglass and Frederick Douglass Jr., the sons of abolitionist Frederick Douglass, also lived in Denver and established the city's first school for African American students.

Around the turn of the last century, many prosperous African American families began to move to Denver's Five Points neighborhood, located northeast of downtown. Built in the 1880s as an upper-class neighborhood, Five Points aimed to attract professionals and business-men and their families. Initially planned as a white neighborhood, an eventual demographic shift transformed Five Points into a vibrant home to six thousand African American Denverites. They occupied the neigh-borhood's stately homes and bungalows and ran businesses, while their children attended classes at the nearby schools.

Five Points was their oasis at a time when de facto segregation and violence against African Americans were still treated as acceptable norms. Although Denver might have been less hostile toward groups such as women, it still wasn't immune from the scourge of racism. In the 1920s, Colorado had an estimated fifty thousand card-carrying members of the Ku Klux Klan. The Klan appears to have had plenty of power of its own, even without the support of law enforcement or local authorities, but documents reveal that membership belonged to plenty of men in positions of power, including judges, a police chief, and even a governor.

The Denver Klan's gnarled roots took firm hold in 1921 at a meeting in the famed Brown Palace Hotel, where eager members and hopefuls lined up to pay dues of $16.50 (a $10 fee and $6.50 for a white sheet and hood) and to craft plans to infiltrate Denver politics. Members wanted to gain representation in high statewide offices, in municipal positions, and in the local police and fire departments.

They succeeded. And with an enabled Klan running organizations and influencing policies, all groups in their crosshairs were subject to bouts of violence, intimidation, and harassment. In addition to the local African American population, the Klan also targeted the Jewish population, Catholic immigrants, and Italians. One law that the Klan supported and nearly helped passed was to prevent the serving of alcohol in church, an obvious swipe at Communion, Catholics in general, and Italian Catholic immigrants in particular.

While the African American community made strides and created more opportunities for themselves, Denver—and the nation, for that matter—continued to sidestep treating all its citizens equally. Nowhere was that more reflected than in de facto racial segregation policies. In 1933, the New Deal was introduced. Praised to this day for its vision and forethought, on paper it was intended to incentivize better living. One program, in theory, included supporting home buying for all Americans, but in practice, it mostly applied to white Americans.

As part of the initiative, the Home Owners Loan Corporation evaluated the risks of issuing mortgages in certain neighborhoods by using a color-coded system. A green neighborhood was considered the "best," while so-called "hazardous" neighborhoods received a red designation. Neighborhoods with an over 71 percent minority population were always designated red.

A designation of red meant it was easier to deny mortgage loans. When introduced, the New Deal's housing initiatives had been designed to bridge mortgage-payment gaps by providing low-interest, long-term mortgages. But it also froze out entire swaths of potential homeowners. To make matters worse, a widely accepted decree in a 1938 manual of the Federal Housing Administration stated: "If a neighborhood is to retain stability, it is necessary that properties shall continue to be occupied by the same social and racial classes."

In the long run, though, these barriers to entry didn't matter in some areas. Greater Denver was growing, and by 1950, 415,786 residents called the sixty-six square miles that comprised metro Denver home. Of that number, a group the Census Bureau lumped together as "nonwhites" numbered 18,252, representing 4.4 percent of the total population.

As Denverites who would one day identify as members of what they called "old Denver," the Mosley family was quite familiar with the navigation of racial segregation. It had sometimes interfered with their goals and dreams when they were younger, but by 1975, things around the nation felt as though they were inching toward more racial equality.

Earlier, in 1954, both eyes and TV cameras had been glued to Supreme Court news coming out of Topeka, Kansas. The landmark ruling in the case *Brown v. Board of Education* initiated the process of desegregating the American public education system. But that ruling had come too late for Edna's husband, John Mosley Jr. Despite his being a National Merit scholar and high school valedictorian, John had attended Colorado State College of Agriculture and the Mechanic Arts (modern-day Colorado State University) as one of nine African American male students. He was not allowed to live in the student housing offered on campus. An aviation enthusiast, he one day would make a family legend of his own after successfully flying a small craft under a bridge between Kansas City and St. Louis with two of their children in the seat behind him, but he would have to fight the armed forces after they attempted to put him in a segregated air unit. Like Edna, for John it was best or bust. And best meant Tuskegee or nothing. Eventually, he won that battle and the armed forces complied.

I paid for my ticket. I'm not moving.

Helena, Arkansas, is famous for two things, one bad and one good. Together they say a lot about the African American experience in the South. The first is a racist massacre during the Red Summer of 1919 when hundreds (the exact number is unknown) of African American residents were murdered by a white mob in nearby Elaine, Arkansas. The fallout from the massacre led to death sentences for twelve African American men for the death of five white participants, but nothing was done about the mass amount of deceased African American men. The defendants were split into two groups: six were known as the Ware defendants, and the other six were known as the Moore defendants. Both groups were ultimately found guilty of murder and sentenced to death, but their communities didn't give up on the fight for justice for them. The Supreme Court intervened on their behalf in 1923 when it heard the case *Moore v. Dempsey*, which appealed the state rulings through federal courts and helped determine if the defendant's constitutional rights were upheld. The case gave the Supreme Court a larger role for intervention in criminal decisions at the state level. Eventually, all twelve men were released.

The second thing Helena is known for is its role in helping to bring blues music to the nation. In 1941, Robert Lockwood Jr., of nearby Turkey Scratch, and Rice Miller, known as Sonny Boy Williamson, approached local Helena radio station KFFA, asking to play their music on the radio. When the local shop Interstate Grocer Co. agreed to sponsor the segment, the show *King Biscuit Time* was born. Airing around lunchtime from 12:15 to 12:30, Monday through Friday, the program was an instant success, with its tagline "Pass the biscuits, 'cause it's *King Biscuit Time*." It was so beloved that flour sales skyrocketed and a cornmeal product named after Sonny Boy Williamson hit the market shortly thereafter. To this day, blues fans return to Phillips County for the annual King Biscuit Blues Festival.

Although she had moved away from the South when she was a teenager, it remained significant to Edna. She still had family there, and it was part of her history. Its place in the civil rights movement would only continue to intensify. A year after she was asked to leave the platform, Money, Mississippi, would become a flashpoint after the violent lynching of fourteen-year-old Emmett Till. His shaken mother, Mamie Till, would order an open-casket funeral and invite the media to come look and take pictures, to show the world what pure, potent Mississippi hatred had done to her child.

Two years later, in 1957, Arkansas would make civil rights–related national headlines courtesy of the Little Rock Nine. This group made news across the globe with footage of them being the first African American students to integrate Little Rock Central High School, facing down a violent mob as they tried to do so.

But back in Helena, Arkansas, in 1954, Edna Mosley was on her own in a place that still bore a blemish for its part of America's racism legacy and surely in a pickle. She had to think fast. What she did next has become the stuff of family legend.

Right there on that platform in Jim Crow–infested Arkansas, with her children in tow, Edna Mosley rooted her feet to the ground. Rather than leave the platform as she had been told, Edna instead addressed that man. And Edna Mosley told him no. She, Edna Mosley, would not move for him. The children, too, would not move for him. Nobody on the platform with the last name Mosley was moving even so much as one inch for that strange white man demanding they leave. *I paid for my ticket. I'm not moving.*

Did she think of John at that moment? How, despite being a star scholar and athlete, he still had to clear unfair hurdles created to slow him down and discourage him and other African American men like him, simply because of the color of their skin? John had gone on to play football for Colorado State. He racked up awards both for playing football and for the school's wrestling team. He was so respected by his peers that they elected him vice president not once but twice, for his junior and senior years there.

She and John were a team. And they didn't have to do anything they didn't want to for anyone. In Helena, as the strange white man waited for her to obey his orders, she might have reasoned to herself that a train was coming, and come hell or fury, these Mosleys were getting on that train. She might have explained that the train was to take them out of Helena and home to Denver. John would be expecting their return, for God's sake.

But what her children heard her saying out loud was something different. And on that day, what she told that strange, demanding man set his rage into motion. She had paid for her ticket, she said, staring at that strange man. Her children had their tickets, too, all paid up in full. They were not moving, she said. Not for him. Not for anyone. Not until that train they had paid their tickets for pulled up to take them out of Helena.

The family legend trails off here, with scant details of what exactly transpired next. But the result was that while standing up for herself and defending her legitimate tickets to board the train, Edna Mosley was arrested. Her refusal to leave the platform proved too much for that strange white man who demanded she leave, and he got the local police involved. She ended up spending a long night in the nearby town jail.

Edna stayed in that jail overnight wearing the same bright-yellow sundress she had put on the morning before in anticipation of the family's return trip. The following morning, her grandfather arrived to post her bail. Edna didn't stop to freshen up this time. Still wearing the same yellow sundress, she collected her children, and they boarded the next train bound for Denver as quickly as they could.

Her decision to return to Denver that day meant she missed her bail hearing at the local courthouse, earning her the designation of "fugitive" in Helena, Arkansas. But this didn't matter to Edna Mosley. Vowing to avoid Helena, she christened herself a fugitive from injustice, and carried on. Carrying on had brought her to this moment in this very room, where she listened and shared, and where what she shared was taken seriously. It was a good sign. If this group meant business, so did she.

CHAPTER 10

Bicentennial

December 31, 1975, 11:50 p.m. (EST)

The coming year had to be better. It just *had* to.

In living rooms across the country, people gathered in front of television sets to watch the well-known New Year's Eve spectacle taking place in New York City's Times Square. Turning their backs on the first half of the 1970s must have felt cathartic for many. In just nine more minutes, as it had done for the past sixty-eight years, the bright, shimmery ball would begin its minute-long descent toward the start of the year 1976.

Below it stood a rain-soaked crowd of nearly thirty-five thousand spectators doing their best to ignore the elements while waiting to count down in unison to the stroke of midnight.

Dick Clark, the night's host, stood nearby in a tan trench coat. Two decades before, he had gained national notoriety as the eternally youthful host of TV's *American Bandstand*. When the camera panned out for live footage of the chilled, sodden mob, he chuckled to the TV audience, musing, "Look at them down there. Wouldn't you just love to be there?"

Nearby, in Philadelphia, to honor the nation's coming bicentennial year, one of the city's most iconic historic artifacts, the Liberty Bell, was to be moved from its location at Independence Hall to a newly constructed viewing center. Initially, Philadelphia expected some fifty thousand spectators to watch the move, but it was raining in Philadelphia, too, and police reported a thinned crowd of about twenty thousand guests.

At nearly two hundred years of age, the US was still a relatively young nation compared to many in the rest of the world, but the past handful of months had been financially sobering and emotionally brutal. Youthful optimism about the future was as cold and damp as the weather on the East Coast that evening. Much of the enthusiasm and hope for 1976 had already soured long before the year itself had begun.

At the prompt stroke of midnight, as red, white, and blue balloons mixed with the rain pouring down on the crowd in New York, it was impossible for anyone to fully exhale with relief about the New Year. While 1976 was brand spanking new, its predecessor, 1975, had proved to be a mixed bag at best. For some, it had been a downright cruel year.

By December 31, families were used to turning on the television set, seeing even more news about the war and the fall of Saigon, and then changing the channel to laugh along with the laugh tracks accompanying controversial Norman Lear shows like *The Jeffersons* or *All in the Family*. Over the summer in New York City, the cast that would later become known as the "not ready for prime-time players" kicked off rehearsals for a brand-new weekend variety show. Called *Saturday Night Live*, it debuted in the fall.

Some felt the nation's core values and moral fiber had begun to unravel. Citing television programming as an influential medium that needed reeling in, at the urging of lobbyists and in the name of family values, networks carved out an official early-evening time slot just after dinnertime. Designating it "family hour," networks agreed to only air programming that was considered suitable for children and adults to watch together. Those paying attention to the pace of hoped-for progress and equality had to wonder whether this new family hour was a harmless change, or did it indicate a return to the more regressive attitudes of the 1950s?

For anyone who'd craved a more even playing field or advocated for justice or equality, 1975 was just another year when powerful, influential men publicly got away with violence, murder, and misbehavior. If it wasn't another thing to pile on the Nixon administration's laundry list, there was always the handful of soldiers who'd remained on trial for their alleged misconduct and subsequent war crimes in the Southeast Asian jungles during the Vietnam War. Viewers could also count on finding trial updates related to the 1970 shooting deaths of four students at Kent State University in Ohio who'd been protesting the Vietnam War. The war might have recently been declared over, but had anything really changed? Cynical skeptics, both young and old, had to wonder.

It was clear Gerald Ford was leading a beleaguered populace. People needed something optimistic to hang on to as they rang in the bicentennial year. They needed to feel that they all shared the same concerns. One couldn't be expected to simply sing "Happy Birthday" to a nation they felt had betrayed them or gotten away with shattering their hopes and dreams. Speaking from the White House, he tried to lift spirits. Meeting with twenty-three reporters in the Oval Office, he shared his vision for 1976.

Ford wanted the nation to move on from its newest round of mistrust in leadership brought on by Nixon's missteps. His prompt pardoning of Richard Nixon had angered those who had expected Nixon to fry for his role in the Watergate scandal. Ford had explained that the pardon was sensible if the country was to heal and move forward. But Ford's words were cold comfort for some.

The nation Ford had taken over was exhausted from the hemorrhaging of resources, prosperity, and optimism. Stanching that bleeding was atop Ford's list of priorities. Helen Thomas of UPI quoted Ford's hopeful dispatch: "I have a vision of what I want America to be," he shared with a roomful of reporters. Ford went on to describe a place where 215 million Americans were "at peace with ourselves." Among other hopes, he pictured peace throughout the world, a strong economy, deeper individual freedoms, and a protected environment. "I get up every morning and can't wait to get to this office to get to the problems," he said. "And I never go home at night feeling we haven't made some progress."

Still, most Americans taking polls about that year didn't share the president's sunny outlook, and worse still, their pessimism wasn't exactly unfounded. The US was supposed to be a global superpower, with the post–World War II boom years having promised prosperity and success were attainable for everyone. All it allegedly took to get there was a willingness to work hard enough, to fall into necessary roles some embraced while others, like LaRae Orullian, had questions. Yet, just two decades later, the goalposts had moved, and working "hard enough" didn't always create a linear path to success. Confidence had waned, in some places to a threadbare status, and well-paying jobs were harder to find. It had been less than two years since the oil embargo had led to shortages, with long lines and high prices at the gas pump and sometimes no fuel because the gas station had run out. It felt like wartime austerity, rather than a boom economy and peacetime prosperity. The fuel crisis had passed, but in 1975, the price of oil had still risen to over $13 per barrel, compared to the average of $12.52 in 1974 and $4.08 just two years before in 1973. There were also the sobering realities of several bankrupt railroads and the bankruptcy announcement by W. T. Grant, a major player in discount department stores.

The latest numbers had inflation at 9 percent, while unemployment numbers danced around after rising from 7.2 percent in December 1974 to 8.1 percent in January 1975. All told, the Ford administration was in the throes of grappling with a recession some labeled the worst since the Great Depression.

During financially hard times, fewer consumers have money to spend on things like new cars. Chrysler faced a 120-day backlog of inventory, with its vehicles starting at around $5,000 for a base trim. To appeal to the inflation-wary American consumer, Chrysler offered incentive rebates to the tune of $200 to $400 to encourage more new cars to be driven off its sales lots.

To tackle the spike in unemployment, Ford introduced a bill that would infuse $5 billion into the extension of unemployment-insurance benefits and assist with public sector jobs programs. Ford also proposed a $16 billion tax cut, which included a rebate of up to $1,000 for individual income taxes paid in 1974. He also called for the release of roughly $2 billion in impounded highway-construction funds. Later, in the spring, the Senate passed a $6.1 billion bill aimed at creating or continuing a million public sector jobs.

All of which is to say, it was not a practical time to open a new, unusual kind of bank. And yet, in October 1975, that's exactly what First Women's Bank in New York had done. With the clever marketing of a portrait of the Mona Lisa in the place where a currency bill might have a man's picture, the bank was ready to get started. Madeline McWhinney, the president of the new bank, made their mission clear: "We are going to prove that many women are good credit risks and represent good business for banks," she told news sources. "But we are not going to make loans to a woman simply because she is a woman."

When First Women's Bank opened its doors in New York City, the event could only be described as a spectacle. Its fresh, remodeled space emphasized glamour, sleekness, and modernism with a bold color palette of forest green, burgundy, rust, and white. Located in the Ritz Tower at 111 East Fifty-Seventh Street, near the corner of Park Avenue, it occupied the same space as the once-famed Le Pavillon restaurant, which had been hailed as the "finest French restaurant in the United States" in the *New York Times* announcement of its closing.

The organizers of this bank had taken pains to consider various women's needs in every aspect of its construction. This included how they designed the space and what materials and items went into the layout. These considerations resulted in moves such as swapping out harsh but traditional fluorescent lighting for a softer, more golden-yellow illumination. The organizers wouldn't need a congressional rep to intervene when it came to pantyhose either. The countertops at their teller stations were deliberately rounded, to help thwart potential pantyhose snags.

In the late 1960s and early 1970s, banking technology had rapidly modernized, thanks to the implementation of digitized systems and automation. Technology set out to streamline systems and bolster convenience for both the bank and its customer. From the beginning of banking's existence, records were a vital part of the process. They needed frequent updates to ensure account accuracy. But the nature of recordkeeping often necessitates an extensive paper trail that can clog up processes. The new banking technology included remarkable, even paperless systems that promised to keep accounts both accurate and safe while reducing some of the heavy reliance on physical paper records. Check processing and bank statements were two paper-intensive banking tasks that early automation set out to revolutionize. Soon, personal trust and commercial loan accounting, credit-card processing machines, and ATM systems would join the new banking-technology lineups.

Revolutionary at the time of its introduction, the ATM allowed the customer to conduct contactless deposits and withdrawals at a stand-alone ATM instead of requiring them to physically walk inside a building and up to a bank teller's window when the bank was open. An option to pay bills using another new technology, the touch-tone phone, was an additional cutting-edge convenience that bank clients enjoyed. Pay by phone made the steps and time it took for check writing, mailing bills, and waiting for a check to clear obsolete. But this convenient new technology and the equipment required to deploy it did not come cheap. In light of the costs, the First Women's Bank group in New York had opted not to purchase every newfangled thing on offer, but they did invest heavily in services they thought would best provide their clients with the conveniences that mattered most to them.

On hand to support the bank on its opening day was famed feminist author and speaker Betty Friedan, who continued to ruffle feathers with her book *The Feminine Mystique*. Friedan was a founder of First Women's Bank. Actress Valerie Harper, who'd captured hearts playing Rhoda, sidekick to single girl extraordinaire Mary Richards on the sitcom *The Mary Tyler Moore Show*, was also there. She had done such a convincing job as Rhoda that the network gave Harper her own show, which was airing at the time of the bank's opening.

The bank was conceptualized by Eileen Preiss, a political organizer who had worked for the George McGovern presidential campaign and devoted countless unpaid hours on behalf of the New York State Democratic Committee. One night at a family dinner, she found herself at a crossroads of sorts. By then, the three Preiss children were mostly grown and out of the house. With McGovern's campaign stumbling, she was becoming disenchanted with politics as a way to enact social change.

One day, she watched her husband, Al, go over a folder of financial materials. "I realized that I didn't even know what was in it," Preiss would later say. Her curiosity about finances at home stretched into curiosity about how other women might be handling their family and personal finances too. While brainstorming at dinner one night, she brought up her idea of starting a women's bank. With her interest piqued, Preiss then reached out to her network of connections to see if they might want to join her and explore the idea more.

New York is never short on powerful, fashionable, stylish women, and many seemed drawn to this institution. Designer Pauline Trigère signed on practically instantly. Preiss resembled Lynda Carter, who played comic book superhero Wonder Woman on television. In one photo spread for an article about Preiss and the bank, she poses in her office, where a portrait of her three children hangs, and in the building's center, where she stands in front of a raised, glassed-in island of sorts, always with her hands in her pockets. Her outfit, a black pantsuit with a shimmery tie-neck blouse, is completed with a pair of large, round, dark sunglasses, while her hair falls in playful, dark waves away from her face. Preiss would always insist that she had no banking experience and that she was strictly there to work on the bank's publicity, marketing, and advertising. But Preiss's lack of experience didn't matter as much as her support did because, in Madeline McWhinney, the bank had *the* ideal candidate to assume the role of president.

At fifty-three, McWhinney was no stranger to the banking world. Growing up in Denver, she had heard plenty of bank-related shop talk, thanks to her banker father. A pedigreed scholar with academic awards, she had graduated from Smith College, one of the East Coast's famed Seven Sisters schools for young women, and had gone on to earn her MBA at New York University. Practical experience would come courtesy of the thirty years she spent working for the Federal Reserve Bank of New York. In her final years with the Fed, she achieved the title of assistant vice president, which officially made her a groundbreaker and the first woman officer there.

One of the last things McWhinney did at the Fed before she left for First Women's Bank was to help design the electronic funds transfer (EFT) system that would later be used nationwide. Like Preiss, McWhinney had a style and an image that were distinct, unmistakable, and often the subject of discussion. She wore her salt-and-pepper hair short and wavy, looking as though she had always just stepped fresh from the beauty salon. Her signature look also often included dark, horn-rimmed glasses and the on-trend ensembles that had become synonymous with a powerful female executive's wardrobe.

As one of only a few early prominent women bankers, McWhinney was often sought out for her advice, which frequently skewed toward topics around personal finance. In a January 1976 *House & Garden* article dedicated to tackling the nation's prevailing inflation problems, she shared her candid opinion. The magazine's mostly female readership was advised to consider growing their own food and, whenever possible, to think about walking instead of using public transit or driving a car. "Adjustments are rough," she said. "But the sooner you realize you have to make them, and once you've made them mentally, you live more easily."

With the local New York City economy cratering by the day even as the bank continued to inch its way closer toward opening, the leadership, which now included McWhinney, made their mission clear: While the bank would seek to serve the needs of women, it would not be exclusive to women. This was a bank that saw green *and* gender. Meaning, men were also more than welcome to open accounts at the bank and to seek out services.

But a festive atmosphere and a well-known celebrity contingent at its glamorous opening couldn't mask a difficult truth that would soon come to light: First Women's Bank was doomed even as it opened. The bank wasn't as robust as its funders and leaders hoped, and it limped along in the months and years after its opening. It is difficult to pinpoint a lone culprit that did the venture in, but even before its grandiose opening, First Women's Bank had cracks in its foundation. These cracks would soon split the venture wide open and expose its problems for critics to examine and pick at.

Raising enough money for an initial stock offering is always a difficult early hurdle to clear. Like with any new venture, it was nearly impossible to time the exact perfect moment for an investor to buy in. When meetings for the New York bank began in 1973, the then-weathered economy looked as though it might be on the upswing and therefore more favorable than it actually turned out to be. The group had initially hoped to raise $4 million from their stock offering but ended up scaling back to $3 million. Stock ultimately sold to small investors for the most part, which McWhinney still considered "quite a feat in the economic climate that we have today. I don't know a bank that isn't having a hard time raising capital."

Stockholders included heavy hitters like Mount Holyoke, Simmons, Smith, and Wellesley Colleges. On its opening day, a reported one thousand people came in to see the bank begin its operations. Three hundred fifty people opened a checking or savings account that day, and *Ms.* magazine, Saks Fifth Avenue, *Vogue*, and Bloomingdale's ceremoniously opened accounts there. One new account holder by day's end was Marina Higgins, a twenty-year-old bookkeeper. She transferred her account, valued at $373.87. Like many women present, she had experienced credit discrimination and could point to her own real-life examples.

Speaking with the press, she shared about the time she wanted to apply for a Macy's Department Store charge card. Macy's had denied her the card on her own, but after she returned with her boyfriend to apply for the same card pretending to be husband and wife, her application was granted. "I just don't think that it's fair that women are treated this way," she said to a *New York Times* reporter who was on hand that day.

Harry Britton, who had made a name for himself as New York City's outspoken "antifeminist 25 cent newspaperman," according to the *New York Times*, hovered at the opening. He stood nearby holding signs with antagonistic messages like "A Woman's Place Is in the Home, Not the Bank."

While Madeline McWhinney and her group set out to open their bank, New York City was busy making dismal financial headlines of its own. In February 1975, news had come down that the city was in an official fiscal crisis and could no longer fund the cost of daily operations. New York also risked defaulting on $792 million in notes that would be due June 11. In July, Mayor Abe Beame proposed an austerity plan that included a wage freeze for city workers, $32 million worth of "nuisance taxes" that aimed to save roughly three thousand city jobs, and the implementation of tuition fees for students attending courses at the City University schools, which, up to then, had been free of charge. Still reeling, on October 29, officials headed to Washington, DC, hat in hand, to request financial help. Ford flat out declined to assist, citing out of control spending as the culprit, which prompted the *New York Daily News* to write the now infamous headline "Ford to City: Drop

Dead." After policy changes in New York, appeals, and pleas, Ford later changed his mind and assisted the city to the tune of $2.3 billion.

A lone financial bright spot for 1975 came during the holiday season after news of a more upbeat consumer-spending trend came through. Consumers might have been beleaguered by all that was going on around them, but high inflation, gas prices, and energy costs and everyday financial pressure weren't going to stop the magic. Spending for Christmas and other winter holidays had remained sacrosanct. Noting that sales during the holiday season of 1975 had risen 17 percent from the same week a year prior, a January 5 *Denver Post* op-ed cautioned, "For some months now, the average consumer has seen unemployment rise, prices increase, relatives, friends (or himself) out of work. The net result has been a reluctance to buy. The US savings average has been an abnormally-high 8 percent."

Holiday sales did little to stem consumers' woes. In a Gallup poll taken on the cusp of the nation's bicentennial year, 85 percent of respondents said they felt that, in 1976, the US was headed for a year of economic troubles. A tenant of Brooks Tower, one of the tallest apartment buildings in Denver, summed up the general sentiment during the holiday season that year when the twinkle lights in their window pointedly quoted Charles Dickens's notorious enemy of Christmas, Ebenezer Scrooge, spelling out the word "humbug" for all of downtown Denver to behold.

If people wavered in their optimism for the coming year, perhaps the opposite could be said for the women's bank group in Denver. Hungry for knowledge and voracious to get it, they had spent the past handful of months chasing down leads and hunting for clues about how to properly form a bank for women. The year hadn't exactly been an economic blockbuster for Denver's economy either. The region, too, had felt financial impacts related to the ongoing energy crisis. Denver also suffered from stalled efforts to revive consumer interest in gold, one of its most abundant resources. Lackluster interest from consumers had a negative impact, but nothing could sway the group from a sense of accomplishment and optimism about the project. They had lived through the exact same year as everyone else and shared similar woes and concerns, but they had set their sights on a solution—the realization of an entirely different goal that was getting closer by the day. And even small steps toward that goal brought along with them more optimism.

Thanks to Carol Green's initial findings and their collective research that year, they had learned plenty about what it took to start a bank. Their feasibility-study results would reveal whether it was too ambitious or if Denver itself was too Wild West to be taken seriously. After speaking to several firms, the group had chosen the firm BB&C Associates to conduct the study. At the stroke of midnight on January 1, 1976, the Denver bank project was still shaping up, even if the progress was at times more tortoise than hare.

They had formalized a few things, compared to when meetings had started that past spring. In addition to taking minutes, they began to hold formal votes around proposed policies and actions. Meetings might be more structured and organized than before, but they still involved the same jovial, lively debates that had always occurred. Things had sharpened up some, though. Now they had more focus. The group also wasn't afraid to have a laugh. On January 9, when they held their first meeting together in 1976 and it came time to read and approve the minutes from the previous meeting, they voted unanimously to skip it because Susanne Bailey, who acted as secretary and had recorded the minutes, wasn't there.

"Susanne's absence means that someone new needs to record these minutes," someone had said.

Looking around at the handful of men and women in attendance that afternoon, pens flicked, paper rustled, and one man chuckled. It was Carol Green's accountant, Mike Feinstein.

"I can take them," he said, nodding. "In order to reverse the normal sex roles."

Smiles spread across the room, and with a click of his pen, Mike was ready to go as the group's temporary secretary for that session.

In good spirits all around, they kicked off their first meeting of 1976, which took place at a woman named Barbara Sudler's palatial home. The agenda items included the need to agree on the bank's name and get an update on group finances.

Since the beginning, the bank's name had been a hotly contested issue. Two distinct camps had formed as a result. There were those who wanted the word "women" or "woman" in the title and those who did not. In addition to the name, the physical location had proved to be a difficult detail to agree on. Some wanted the bank to be part of the downtown scene, while others cautioned the group not to overlook the city's outposts and its outskirts.

What wasn't tricky to navigate that day, however, was where the finances stood. As it turned out, they were in pretty decent shape. Monies broke down as follows:

- $21,000 in initial member contributions
- –$2,000 in refunds to two original members who had departed
- –$5,000 for attorney's fees
- –$2,000 to the firm of BB&C Associates for consulting fees

This left them with a fairly robust balance of $12,000 to work with. A shoestring budget could stretch that money some, they hoped.

The nation might have been feeling a financial squeeze right at that moment, but in Denver, those who believed in the bank project left the meeting after five o'clock feeling ready to take on the next set of challenges. Some might have even said they felt downright optimistic.

Their sense of quiet contentment, however, would not last.

CHAPTER 11

The Ceiling

How does a woman become eligible to run a bank?

In the more than twenty years since she'd first moved to Denver, LaRae Orullian had become *the* woman in town you could ask, because she was the one who surely knew. She had mastered the art and craft of banking—just like she had memorized the feel of wrapping pennies back in Salt Lake. By the 1970s, her banking skill set had come courtesy of both education and absorption through daily osmosis over more than two decades in her career. She was fluent in the inner workings and quirks of banks. By now, there was precious little about running a bank that LaRae didn't know. Whether it was how to make great coffee she'd never even tasted, because faith in her Mormon upbringing remained ingrained in her, or how to write a loan, or anything in between.

The 1950s remained a somewhat sleepy era when considered in hindsight or even through the lens of nostalgia. But it was in the 1950s that some seeds of change for women's roles and positions had been planted and began to grow. They wouldn't fully bloom for several years, but 1954 turned out to be as important for the nation's women as it had been for LaRae Orullian. The perfect housewife and mother stereotype might have played out on TV, but while that droned on, women had begun to flex their increasingly powerful muscles in the political arena. In January, a memo from Mrs. J. Ramsay Harris of the National Citizens for Eisenhower Congressional Committee revealed that it had been women who won him the election. They had given him 58.1 percent of their vote, which was nearly 6 percent more than their male counterparts had done, at 52.7 percent. The memo also revealed that 19 million women worked outside their homes. In Denver, twenty-two hundred women's clubs flourished. "The majority of these are study groups [on national affairs]," wrote Harris, "showing that women recognize that a homemaker today is also a citizen." Despite the glossy personas of stay-at-home mothers chasing after broods of children, grocery shopping, and hosting "coffee klatches" in their dream homes, outside interests continued to grab women's attention and to push them.

Harris urged Eisenhower to address himself exclusively to women, advising, "Women do not think as men do. The approach to women should be quite different as evidenced by the Women's Page in every newspaper, women's telecasts, what women's newscasters report to their audiences." On the financial front, Harris noted a new program that the "stock market directs specifically to women in recognition of the fact that women own 45% of all stocks. Note, too, that women (perhaps because they marry younger and live longer) have 70% of the wealth."

Harris's advice to Eisenhower based on her findings further proved that landmark changes for women lay just up ahead on the horizon. And in that landscape, LaRae Orullian found herself in the position of unexpected career trailblazer. After her arrival in Denver, LaRae had almost immediately taken a job at a local bank. By 1976, she still hadn't packed up and headed to New York City and Wall Street as intended. She hadn't even gotten over to Omaha. Both had once been in her plans, but something in Denver had clicked for her almost immediately. So she chose to stay out west and instead put down some roots. About a year after her arrival, LaRae switched jobs, moving to the then newly opened Guaranty Bank. She'd worked there for so long that it would be understandable for her to forget just how long it had actually been. But a woman with a good head for numbers never does.

In those early days on the other side of the Rockies, it had been hard to imagine time or its swift passage. But somehow, while she sat at her desk, her twenties and thirties had flown past her. In that time, seasons changed, people married and made homes, babies were born, folks died. Wars were waged and ended, and their embers continued to smolder. Elvis took the world by storm, followed by The Beatles. Dick Clark took heat for integrating the music and the audience on *American Bandstand*. President John F. Kennedy was assassinated, followed by his brother Robert. The civil rights movement, complete with marches, sit-ins, and protests, became mainstream. Martin Luther King Jr. was assassinated, as was his sometimes possible rival and fellow civil rights activist Malcolm X.

An entire social and pop-culture evolution took place, changing the nation's very face and fabric. And it all happened while LaRae carried on at Guaranty. Career women could also recall going from a skirts-and-dresses-only dress code to the occasional slacks and blouse or pantsuit ensemble being more acceptable.

In addition to a promising career in banking, it turned out that Denver offered LaRae both a life and a community. She took advantage of local opportunities to socialize and could be found playing softball and golf in the warmer weather or hitting the nearby slopes for skiing when the fresh Rocky Mountain powder beckoned. She also enjoyed growing things and thoroughly welcomed opportunities to change out of her work clothes and into a different uniform to then putter around in her garden. Most of these activities took place in her spare time, which was admittedly in short supply.

At the outset, LaRae understood that if she wanted to get ahead in banking, she would need to deepen both her knowledge and her expertise. Almost immediately, she had begun taking night and correspondence courses in banking. This educational pathway took her considerably longer than being a full-time student would have, since she still had her full-time shifts to cover at Guaranty. Thanks to her razor-sharp mind, LaRae slowly began to earn accolades and specialized degrees in banking.

By the time her name appeared in the article that had circulated around Carol Green's living room, LaRae had rightfully earned a position that job descriptions sometimes call "commensurate with talent and experience." Just two years earlier, she was a vice president and secretary to the board at Guaranty. Career-wise, 1975 had been a groundbreaking year. She was selected as one of fourteen managers in banking nationwide to run training programs and seminars for other women working in banking. The goal of the seminars was to help these women "upgrade their skills to be eligible for management and senior management levels." She traveled to Miami and Chicago to attend the trainings and then returned to Denver to put what she had learned into practice.

"Miss LaRae," as she was warmly referred to by clients at Guaranty, had also become a customer favorite over the years. Her encyclopedic knowledge combined with her gentle sense of humor, soft-spoken voice, twinkling eyes, and penchant for career-woman fashion (lots of blues with an occasional print) made her a calm, wise, and respected presence at the bank.

Her appointment to the board of directors at Guaranty in February 1975 was a rare occurrence. It was also unlike the high positions that a few other women held at banks because her appointment was not inherited. She had gained it based solely on her merit. In being promoted to the highest position in banking that a woman in Denver could hold, she had proved it was possible. A woman could roll up her sleeves, get to work, and rise in the ranks at a male-dominated bank. The problem now, though, was that LaRae also knew she was talented and had a pretty good grasp on the value of her work. She could do the same work as a man, and she wanted to go higher, with the salary and title to match her skills.

Still, she wanted a position in that aspirational place she had once nicknamed Mahogany Row all those years ago. Her titles might have changed, but they were not to the level she knew she was capable of.

That deeper longing for more never really went away. LaRae also understood the dilemma behind carrying the weight of her position as the only woman of that stature. While she was grateful for the opportunity, the longing she felt professionally was starting to fray the limited status of the position for her.

With an increasing number of women entering the workforce, banking was a natural fit for many. In Denver, 60 to 70 percent of banking's employees were women, often taking positions at the teller's window or down in a cavernous basement counting room. But customers coming into Guaranty looking for LaRae knew they might find her somewhere in the spaces where decisions were being made. At forty-one, LaRae had achieved the niche position of bank officer, which was only held by 2 or 3 percent of women working in banking. This small number of officers also meant that even though women outnumbered men as bank workers, they mostly all held subordinate positions. In other words, most of the bank's tellers and other support staff might be women, but Mahogany Row was still disproportionately populated by men.

Fair promotion of women to positions they were demonstrably qualified for mattered to LaRae. Not just for herself, but for the other eligible women filling up job vacancies at banks everywhere. The perceived or real lack of eligible, qualified women workers at the top bothered her. It was something she discussed with other women bankers at gatherings for the National Association of Bank Women (NABW), where she was the newly elected president, or at training seminars that she attended with a handful of other female bank manager peers. It was nice not to be the only woman in the room for once, but surely there were more than fourteen of them in the whole country who could run things.

A promotion like hers at Guaranty was a long time coming. It bothered her that men were often automatically assumed to be more capable or qualified as management personnel than she was. Sure, she knew banks on a surface level, their every inch, nook, and cranny. She was fluent in the different sounds they made throughout the day and the particular smells their different rooms and sections held. The lobby, for instance, wouldn't smell like the board room, where coffee and cigars often scented the room. She knew when to expect a lull in foot traffic or when to prepare for a coming rush of customers.

Beyond inner workings, though, LaRae had become a viable candidate whom the men could and would call on to perform tasks for what is now sometimes called "scope creep." In her case, it meant that when there was a dilemma the men in charge couldn't seem to fix, they appealed to her to come and help them out. Sometimes she was pulled in to help sort out bad loans she hadn't even written. Their bad loans became hers to assess, to clean up, to resolve. Scope creep meant their mistakes were easily punted over to her, and ever the team player, she'd help to yet again resolve the issue.

It wasn't that these men whom she helped were ungrateful to her. Most *were* grateful, and some even praised her for her talents. But that gratitude and praise always seemed to stop short of securing the position she wanted and felt eligible to pursue. She wanted to be president. Eventually, it seemed that the men at Guaranty could count on LaRae's help with their messes as much as she could count on watching as Guaranty promoted men who were junior to her to positions higher than hers. Men she had often trained. Sometimes, despite their leveling up, they might still need her skill set to fix their issues. What LaRae *wanted* at work more than anything else was to finally be put in charge of running this bank. If she mentioned her longing—spoke it aloud— she knew she wouldn't be alone. From across the room, whether it was at Guaranty or an NABW meeting, she was met with recognition from other women who felt it too.

These women, too, wanted more.

Still, some recognition—any recognition, for that matter—was better than none at all. Over the years, Guaranty's assets had grown to $66 million, and she had been an integral part of the team making it happen. By the time she sat with *Colorado Business Magazine* to discuss her latest promotion, it was a source of great pride for her.

"Women have to be more aggressive," she advised. Women who waited quietly for a promotion were less likely to get it in the end, because action was needed. She recalled one address to a seminar of bank women where she'd asked how many in the room had approached their employer for a raise. Of the few with their hands up, she'd asked another question:

"Did you get the raise?"

As it turned out, several of them had. If that wasn't proof you had to ask for what you wanted, LaRae didn't know what was.

CHAPTER 12

Judi

Even to this day, Judith "Judi" Foster (now Wagner) swears up and down that she had only joined the group because she adored the idea of women setting up something financial in nature and with women in charge. She hadn't joined to become chair of the Women's Association and a spokeswoman. She attended her first meetings right around Valentine's Day 1976, as the group was finalizing specifics around their charter-application plans. She might have arrived to get more information about becoming involved with the project, but before too long, she would end up becoming a full-fledged leader. It all began at what most thought would be a routine meeting on February 14.

With the exception of the three guests in attendance, it's likely that everyone else in the room had paid their initial $1,000 commitment to be part of the project. Judi was one of the youngest in the group, and although relatively new to it, she'd first heard about the ongoing project at a recent holiday party, and her interest had grown since then. She was a natural fit for the project and the group given her experience working in the world of Denver finance.

Judi had gotten into finance almost on a lark. Born in 1943 to parents who had been high school sweethearts, both of whom had attended college, Judi spent her earliest years moving up and down the East Coast for her father's career assignments with the armed forces. During an exercise, he sustained an injury that sidelined his career, and at age four, several monumental events changed her life. One was the birth of her sister, Wendy, who was premature and would need therapy to assist with her development. Another was that the family relocated to California, settling on a family farm in Barstow. Her grandfather was an orchardist, and Judi spent her time shaped by the ins and outs of growing, tending, and harvesting from the many peach, almond, apricot, and fig trees that grew on the family property.

That same year, her father took her to the local bank to open up a passbook savings account. On the day she walked up to the bank with her father, Judi remembers thinking maybe it was someone's house and wondering to herself what people might live in such a big home. Once inside, her curiosity about the building's occupants gave way to surprise and delight after someone working there explained what a savings account was.

Holding her passbook in her tiny hand, she listened attentively while the banker told her about something she'd never heard of before called "interest."

Free money? The moment she learned of it, Judi knew she liked the concept.

At age seven, Judi's family moved away from the farm and into Fresno. Before long, she found a passion and talent for swimming after her father built the family a pool. Judi showed strength as a swimmer in the butterfly and breaststroke. When she was eleven, she began to compete and eventually lettered in the sport, garnering the honor of being a San Joaquin Valley champion in breaststroke.

When Judi reached high school, her favorite instructor was the journalism teacher. After asking if she could join the school newspaper, she learned she first had to be able to type. She took typing and became fast and good at it, thinking maybe she could one day major in journalism.

In her family, the next logical step after high school was college. Family tradition had been that the girls went to the University of Washington. Upon graduation from high school, despite getting into Berkeley as well, she followed in the footsteps of the women before her and attended the University of Washington, majoring in history with an economics minor.

Throughout her teen and college years, Judi had also made herself tidy sums of money working as a pool manager, lifeguard, and swimming teacher. With the same joy that the notion of free money had brought her at age four still on her mind, Judi continued to make sure to deposit nearly everything she earned into that same savings account. The summer the pretty, petite, fashionable, blue-eyed California girl graduated from college, she promptly put career plans on hold to travel abroad. In Amsterdam, she joined up with three college friends, and the foursome made good on their plans to pick up a Volkswagen bus that had shipped separately from the US and drive together through Europe. They christened the bus Charlie.

Each girl had $1,000 of her own money to contribute to the trip. As a new grad with her own money and few strings attached, Judi didn't have many worries that season, save for how she'd best stretch and grow her money and when or if there might be enough good snow on the nearby slopes to merit a ski trip. For nearly a year, the foursome traveled across Europe aboard Charlie.

When the Europe trip ended, Judi returned to the States and found herself unsure about a next move. After efforts to find work in Seattle as a swim instructor stalled, she furthered her education, getting certified in physical education (PE) with the hopes of becoming a PE teacher. When the Seattle job market proved fruitless for her, she returned to Fresno, where she taught PE.

For a friend's wedding, Judi was set up with a handsome bachelor working toward his PhD who served as her escort. They got along well and, ultimately, fell in love. They agreed that their natural next move was to get married and they did.

After marriage, many newlyweds would presumably start a family and take up the expected roles of breadwinner father and homemaker mother. But, just as she had done after college graduation, Judi took another detour and put the role of homemaker mother on indefinite hold.

Teaching gave her the summers off, and one year, a friend who worked as a small-cap stockbroker asked if she might be interested in learning more about the business. After she agreed, he put her to work, teaching her about both investment portfolios and investment management. It was just like when she learned about interest all those years ago as a child. She not only deeply understood investing as a topic, she also liked it.

In 1968, her husband found work in St. Louis, and they moved there for a year-long stint. While living in Missouri, Judi founded her business, Midwest Associates, a financial firm that focused on investment research and reports.

Even though she owned the business outright, she understood that a woman putting "owner" on anything career-wise related to financial services posed a risk. Such a title might scare off potential customers even if it was true. To appear less ambitious and avoid turning away potential clients, she toned things down a bit and voluntarily demoted herself. As a result, when she passed out business cards, her title was listed as "Vice President" instead of her correct title, which was, in fact, owner and sole proprietor.

Downplaying or downgrading titles was not new. It was a common enough practice for women at that time. Even now, we still don't have to go far to see lasting examples. Many of us repeat the line "stay gold, Ponyboy," but what's less commonly known is that author Susan Eloise "S. E." Hinton was a teen at the time she wrote those words, published in her book *The Outsiders*. Now considered the godmother of young-adult novels, she used her initials in place of her full name to downplay both her age and the fact that she was female. Like S. E. Hinton, Judi was part of the young generation of men and women on the cusp of intense social change. But in 1968, second-wave feminism still had yet to be fully realized.

In Missouri, Judi had listened to feminist icon Gloria Steinem speak at a nearby college. Steinem's message of the coming women's revolution inspired her a great deal. She would go on to become an outspoken feminist. When their year in Missouri ended, she and her husband moved to Denver, where she took work at Boettcher & Company, a legacy financial firm.

Boettcher, as it was often referred to, was both a financial powerhouse and a Denver success story. The surname Boettcher had long been synonymous with entrepreneurship. Started by two German immigrant brothers as a hardware store in 1869, Boettcher grew into a string of stores. The company went public in 1944, and they opened Boettcher Investment in 1962.

Working at the company had gone fine for Judi until one fateful holiday party when a partner let it slip that he would never, under any circumstances, let a woman be a partner in the company.

Even as he uttered his opinion, much was changing for women in their work lives. There were now enforceable laws in place intended to protect women from unfair labor practices. It was also clear, however, that the laws on the books might not scare the partner into compliance. Not then. Or possibly ever.

Judi was good at math. She was pretty sure that spending her career working at a place where male partners were unafraid to hold women back professionally was a dead end for her. A career should give opportunities to rise in the ranks, but Boettcher hadn't exactly panned out as she'd hoped. If she wanted more for herself in the career department, Judi would have to hatch a new plan. Around that same time, she attended another holiday party, where she struck up a conversation with a woman who was with a group of women looking to start up a women's bank.

The first meeting she'd attended impressed her, and here she was, listening in as something seemed to be stirring. Something that, quite frankly, wasn't looking too good.

CHAPTER 13

The Rift

February 14, 1976

Of all the days in the year, a big, smashing disagreement would just have to happen on Valentine's Day, now wouldn't it?

It was nearly a year since Carol Green had first picked up the phone to call her banker and find out whether a woman running a bank in Denver was possible. And, suddenly, here she was, dressed to the nines, ready to start the meeting, and about to throw a rather sizable wrench.

Carol Green was about to resign from her own group—in protest. In this moment, she'd had enough. The sidebar murmurings and chatter about her by some members had intensified to the point that she was ready to leave it all behind and depart. And she also wanted her money back. She couldn't get her time back, all those months she'd spent looking into the project, but hopefully her money was a reasonable request on the way out the door.

Given the often united, enthusiastic spirits within the group up to this moment, it would have been impossible to foresee something this drastic unfolding as it had. There had always been differing personalities and opinions on display stretching as far back as the first meetings. But a general sense of agreement prevailed and even won out when personalities or opinions differed. The common goal to set up the bank always came first.

But everyone has a breaking point. Even the best of intentions can frazzle. A well-intended wish to satisfy all tastes can prove difficult for even the most skilled chef or party host. How much harder, then, is it to tackle the same feat with one's time, personal equity, or maybe even a bit of ego on the line?

Carol Green was about to help everyone find out.

If they were being honest with themselves, looking back, the real trouble had begun long before today. There to document what happened during these particular meetings was their on-again, off-again scribe, Barbara Sudler.

Although she'd been present at most of the meetings of record, Barbara hadn't stepped into the role of secretary immediately. On January 16, 1976, she'd cocreated the meeting minutes with another member, Susan Treadway. But by February 14, when things began to slide sideways, she had been elevated to the role of secretary pro tempore, and she was taking the official notes that helped to document the rift in sketches and broad strokes.

Barbara was the perfect fit for this position, given her penchant for all things linguistic.

As a young woman, Barbara had loved two things passionately, literary pursuits and Colorado's magical scenery. When her father's work brought her family to Denver full time, she grew up there, eventually graduating in 1944 with an English literature degree from the University of Colorado Boulder. Later, she married Jim Sudler, a local architect, and became involved in Denver society. Jim's work at the Denver Art Museum brought Barbara into the same social circles as Betty Freedman. They might run into each other at events like a soiree for the Public Library, where Barbara served as vice president of the foundation at one time, or the Denver Symphony Orchestra. And, like Betty Freedman, Barbara wrote book reviews for the *Denver Post*.

And now here they both were, working together on a committee for a different cause they both believed in. But the bank for women idea found itself in a room fraught with tension that day. Just before Carol Green resigned, Barbara had gently recapped events. And it had been Barbara who said immediately afterward, "I move that we discuss decision-making and delegation of authority."

Within the group, the decision-making and delegation of authority had suddenly become elephants in the room. They would continue to underscore the coming days, growing to a fever pitch, with the role of chairperson rotating among members frequently. At an ad hoc meeting held on February 15, Lynn Hubanks—notably, not Carol Green—sat in the position of chairperson and promptly offered to resign, "so the group can select its chair by election."

The day before, things had begun to unravel quickly, as evidenced by how dramatically the tone in the room shifted after Carol Green requested the floor.

"I'm resigning," she said flatly. "I would like my name completely withdrawn from the group, and my funds returned to me."

A stunned silence filled the room. It would be the last time silence reigned supreme for several days. But Carol wasn't finished just yet.

Attendees looked at one another with confusion. People whispered back and forth, while others swapped bewildered glances. Ultimately, everyone wanted to know why she was leaving.

Nobody needed to prod Carol too hard to get the answers to their questions. She readily offered up her why. "I have several reasons, including the lack of trust in me demonstrated at recent meetings," she said. "I can't continue to be in an association with people who don't trust me."

Her concerns made sense. Trust had become a thorny issue between two of the least likely candidates in the group: Bonnie and Carol. As Barbara took notes, she remembered clear as a bell the January 30 meeting at her home, when Carol had brought up the issue of control of the bank stock. Was that when the problems between the two women really began to brew? It must have been of some kind of significance because in a letter of clarification that she distributed to members on February 10, Carol had written:

> The statement of control of the stock is confusing. What was stated was that there are undoubtedly sufficient members in the group at this time to buy the shares, or to sell them personally. We probably could avoid the biggest problem that other women's banks have faced, the difficult sale of stock. Also, we could avoid the costs of an agent representing us in this matter, if all shares are sold promptly.

Control. It heated the center of the initial disagreement between the two women, who had otherwise gotten along, then it ricocheted outward. Bonnie had come aboard early on because she liked the idea of starting a bank or financial institution for women by women. She envisioned an entity that extended services to as many underbanked and underserved people in Denver as possible. Others weren't as sure as she that the entire underbanked population was the target demographic. Women were risky as it was, and an all-inclusive operation chanced insolvency. As time passed, Bonnie had even begun to have her doubts about whether the project would actually be for and by women. Or if it was women specific, which women *specifically* would it benefit?

Beyond doubting the "by" and "for" women aspects, she had also begun to suspect to herself that the project might be something Carol was doing more for her own benefit and less to benefit women overall. Whether real or unfounded, Bonnie's suspicions grew as time passed. She empathized with women who needed access to credit and banking services and felt deeply that every woman who came in should be allowed to invest in the bank or have access to money. In a separate meeting she had held with, ironically, a male bank president, Bonnie had presented her case regarding limited bank stock ownership stakes, asking if he might help her draft a motion for the charter to limit own-ership stakes for individuals and entities.

Bonnie's motive had been to continue her mission to ensure that if and when the bank was set up, it would actually serve customers and its community, rather than a roomful of stockholders. But in setting up her motion, Bonnie would create a firestorm. That firestorm carved a deep wound into Carol Green's heart, something she would never forget.

In a bit of irony, though, when it came to ownership, whether any one person wanted to own a large percentage of the bank was moot. Limitations around how much stock could be owned already existed. As evidenced by New York City's First Women's Bank, which had opened a few months prior under a state charter, ownership stakes were clearly defined. In the case of New York, the state charter mandated that each investor was limited to a maximum stake of 2.5 percent of the total stock subscription. This meant that no majority stakeholders existed in the New York bank project.

In Carol's note, which reads as more of an inquiry than a decree, she queried the lower percentage as a hindrance. The limited ownership, she explained, "presented a problem to this bank as they did not have enough investors who could invest this amount, although they could have gotten a few investors to buy larger amounts." If the group went with a national charter, each investor would be permitted a maximum of 5 percent of the shares.

Despite trying to keep emotion away from the center and the proj-ect progressing as an all-business venture, emotional cracks formed. With less to lose than others in the group, given her status as a woman who ran her own business, Carol Green had entered the project whole-heartedly and with good intentions. Now she didn't even want her name to be on record. Carol Green felt mistrusted after all this time with the group. She wanted out permanently and immediately.

After several longtime attendees expressed their regretful acceptance of her resignation, the discussion then turned to whether Carol's money could be refunded as she requested. Up to then, most attendees who had paid to be in the group were sticking with the project. With the exception of a couple of departures early on, very few had actually left outright.

Barbara listened as attendees expressed concerns about how withdrawal from the group could or should play out. Refunds weren't something they had planned for or expected to encounter up until now. They could agree that members should be allowed to withdraw, but refunds were something else entirely to grapple with.

Barbara took notes furiously. She already knew these would be important minutes, and longer than usual. She didn't have time to look up as she heard one woman say, "I've inquired about this specific question. I was told I could leave, but I couldn't take any money."

"Listen, Carol. The bottom line is that you are a valued member of the group," Barbara heard someone else say, while the group echoed yeses and mm-hmms. "You are welcome to reconsider your resignation and return."

While Carol mulled that over, there was still the matter of electing a new chairperson because Carol had resigned. Judi had moved for Lynn Hubanks to ascend to the position. It was a motion that passed unanimously.

CHAPTER 14

The Aftermath

We have formed the Association to take whatever steps are
necessary and within our power to the end that a National
Bank Charter is granted and a bank is established in downtown Denver, named Women's Bank, NA. We intend that
this be a full service bank to serve the needs of all persons
equally with a special consciousness of the needs of and
the intent to create opportunities for women. We believe
that women must participate to a greater extent than they
heretofore have in the economic structure of society. We
intend that, in accord with sound banking principles,
the Women's Bank be a catalyst for the expanding role
of women in business, finance, the professions and public life. We intend that Women's Bank serve the financial
needs of women, minorities, and all persons who may have
heretofore been denied bank services and participation in
the financial life of our society because of their race, religion, sex, color, national origin, age and/or marital status.
We further intend that the Women's Bank place special
emphasis on financial counseling for all who wish it and
help the young, single, divorced, widowed, or married person establish a credit pattern.

President: Judith Foster

Vice President: Betty Freedman
Secretary: Barbara Sudler
Treasurer: Mike Feinstein
—Summary of corporate form, August 1976

Although the Denver bank's Women's Association was officially created by the group on November 16, 1975, it was formally solidified on paper following the rift and subsequent fallout in February 1976.

The rift would prove to be more than just a test of group mettle. Meeting after meeting throughout February would show how Carol Green and Bonnie Andrikopoulos represented two different ideologies, and it clearly was time for the group to pick one. Despite her shocking resignation early in the rift, Carol continued to attend meetings during the aftermath. She remained focused on making the bank a success, unlike the cautionary tale of other specialty banks that had gone bust. Her vision was a bank for women that employed as many women as possible and that offered clients in need with services that included credit counseling, but it would ultimately need to be a successful bank. Idealism aside, a successful bank still required adherence to protocols and attraction of the right investors and customers.

Bonnie, in turn, wanted to start a bank that served women, minorities, and the poor. Making the bank a success was secondary to her, and less important than the "by women, for women" ethos. In the aftermath of the rift, the valid concerns of both women bubbled up to the forefront. Although they were uncomfortable and difficult to get through, these disagreements were still invaluable. They meant it was time to get more official about what exactly the group wanted to do and how they wanted to proceed. There's nothing like a crisis, after all, to focus the mind. Whom did they want to serve? What was the target demographic? Logistics lingered in the air above them. They had to be clear now and agree to be in lockstep. Once they came to a consensus about what the project would truly be and whom it would serve, there could be no turning back.

With tension still running high, at a meeting on February 23, which would be the final time she spent with the group, Bonnie and some members who planned to leave with her were present. This time, she sat in the still-rotating position of chairperson. There was so much on the line now. Each side had valid reasons for their points of view, and neither was ready to cede their ground. Following the review of previous meeting minutes, Jessica Luna and Lynn Hubanks, who had been part of the rift and had sided with Bonnie, asked to share a prepared statement. It was immediately ruled out of order as "an insertion in previous minutes." Overall group tension just after reading the minutes didn't exactly signal a peaceful start to things.

By now, Barbara and Betty believed in this project wholeheartedly and were determined to see it through. Both women had watched as previous meetings unfolded, only to veer sharply and go sideways. Chatter exploded around them; all concerns were entertained, and voices needed to be heard. But any experienced committee member like Barbara or Betty knew that sometimes, when it's time to press on, the tug-of-war between sides must conclude. Something had to give. Often, the right way to get things fixed in moments like this was to smooth ruffled feathers and get past the prickles that had surfaced. It was time to support a leadership team with the ability to get the project back on track.

At that moment, "back on track" also meant appointing a proper leader who could navigate the project at hand. That leader would need to recognize the different personalities within and without the group. They needed someone who could lead right away and without emotion or prior baggage. Someone who was not a main character in the rift.

"I move that we nominate an impartial person to occupy the position of chairperson," said Norma Besant, who had been at the fraught February meetings.

"I second the motion," said Betty. It was as though Norma had read her mind. Going forward, neither Carol nor Bonnie could occupy the seat. It wasn't recorded who exactly nominated her, but newcomer

Judi Foster suddenly found herself a candidate for the position of chairperson; before she could let the nomination sink in, the motion was immediately passed.

With enough "ayes" around the room, it was settled. Judi Foster was the nomination for chairperson. And if voted in, what a group mess she'd inherit and have to clean up.

Although she hadn't been part of the group for more than a few meetings, other members had already been impressed by her. And her résumé didn't hurt either: Judi was a security analyst and registered investment advisor. She understood the language of money and finance. Before she could fully process what was going on, a surprised Judi was then elected to the position of chairperson by a landslide.

Eventually, the discussion had to return to the thorny dilemma of bank stock ownership. Anyone present during the last few tumultuous meetings knew firsthand that part of the rift was about this very subject. Specifically, how much stock should any one member or family unit be permitted to own. Percentages mattered, because percentages equaled power when it came to policy and decision-making. Bonnie felt Carol wanted to own a majority share, which was more stock than anyone ought to have. Meanwhile, Carol pointed to the very tangible issue of how difficult it had been for New York City's First Women's Bank to sell enough of its stock. If members were allowed to own more stock outright, generating outside interest wouldn't be as much of a driver for selling stock, and there would be potentially less to sell and possibly even less at the mercy of yet-to-be-discovered investors who might or might not buy bank stock at all.

At some point during these days, things had gotten so heated that even Judi had begun to lose faith in whether they could continue working together. During one meeting, she had even found herself hitching her petite frame up on top of the conference room table and raising her voice over the din to call for peace and order after the room erupted into explosive debate.

Both Carol and Bonnie had valid points. But as it turned out, any fears about who could own what and how much or about having to sell enough stock to outside investors wouldn't matter in the long run. If they wanted to be nationally chartered and to earn the "NA" designation, the rules were clear.

Lawyer Juereta Smith, who had spent some time examining documents and rules, had the definitive answer. "Ownership of stock should be as broadly based as feasible, with no family unit owning more than five percent," she said. That settled it. Whether they were going for a national or a state charter, there would be no majority stakes permitted within the founding membership. If they went with the national charter, for instance, any family could buy up to 5 percent but no more than that. Which meant that "John Public" couldn't buy 5 percent if his wife, "Jane," already owned 5 percent.

The rule made sense, and thankfully, it would end any potential future back-and-forth about the matter. "I would like to propose we add 'in accordance with sound banking practices,'" Dore Leiser suggested. They wanted to follow sound banking practices, and because they were tilting more toward a national charter, if it was granted, stock ownership of 5 percent or less would be the group's gospel.

All around the room, heads nodded, but when it came to the floor for a vote, five members abstained from voting at all.

Judi looked toward the five members who'd just said a lot by saying nothing. "I'd like to discuss the philosophical split we have here," she said in her first action on record as chairperson. It was time to take the bull by the horns.

It turned out that the abstention group disagreed with and took aim at the preincorporation agreement that Juereta Smith had just summarized.

Personal opinions couldn't override protocols, though. It was time to look toward another attorney in the room. "Tenn," Judi asked one of their lawyers, "can you tell us what you advise here?"

"A preincorporation agreement isn't usual, but this is not a usual bank charter," he said. "Bank regulators like wording like 'sound banking practices.'"

Somewhere in the room, someone lit a cigarette and exhaled emphatically.

The real split was coming.

"Because of the irreconcilable differences, I move that the larger of the two philosophical groups assume the liabilities of the Women's Association," Carol proposed. "Further, I move that the group vote on issues like the incorporators and the executive committee and that those who cannot live with these decisions be fully reimbursed, unless withdrawal is so large that we can't prorate the funds. At which time, we can entertain a motion to dissolve the group entirely."

"We also need to nominate people who are willing to serve, and they need to share their qualifications with the group. They must be able to pass inspection by the comptroller," Susanne Bailey added. The motion carried.

Aside from abstaining earlier in the meeting, Dave Jennings had been unusually quiet. In past meetings, he had been a rather vocal presence. He could be counted on to debate potential bank names or locations and not to always waver in his position. Something was up. This time, Dave, along with Bonnie, Lynn Hubanks, and Jessica Luna, was ready to get his final word in. "On behalf of Bonnie, Lynn, and Jessica, I move that all four of us be allowed to resign."

The room was silent and still for a moment until the heft of what he said sank in.

With nearby eyes widening, Lynn Hubanks spoke next. "I move that all four of us be allowed to resign and be bought out."

"Second," Jessica Luna added. Just a few days earlier, it had been Carol Green looking to resign and get her money back. She had been persuaded to stay put. The foursome now seeking to exit posed a different challenge—a $4,000 withdrawal from the group funds if their wishes were granted.

The motion was withdrawn almost immediately. Refunds and buy-outs hadn't yet been sorted out among the group. Any agreement to pay out any money now, without further discussion, could prove to be a costly mistake.

Looking at each other, the foursome threw in their final plea for the evening. They'd take money off the table for now, but they still wanted out. "I move that our four resignations be accepted tonight," said Lynn.

"Second," Bonnie said almost immediately.

The motion carried. In the minutes for the meeting, Barbara Sudler labeled this section "resignations accepted with regret."

Mike Feinstein then took the floor. If those departing wanted their money back, the group could surely try to work something out. It was time for a gesture of good faith. "I move that every effort be made to refund the resignees' capital investment," he said. Susanne Bailey seconded.

With that out of the way, the newly resigned foursome rose from their seats and departed from the room. Another stunned silence fell over the fourteen remaining meeting attendees. Some shifted uncomfortably and others whispered quietly to their neighbors.

With the splinter group gone for good, it was time for anyone left in the room to truly and honestly recommit to the project. If there were any other fears or hesitancies, they needed to be addressed head-on before the group conducted any other formal business about the bank. The clock was already ticking on this project. In just a few short days, they would formally apply to the comptroller for a nationally chartered bank with the word "women" in its name.

Betty spoke first of the formal elections. "I move that we elect the interim board members."

"Seconded," said Barbara.

The motion carried.

"For the bank's incorporators," Tenn said, "some of you now on the interim board should be appointed." The incorporators would apply for the charter, sit for the test, and serve as the names and representatives on the application to organize.

Upon their attorney's advice, Betty, Judi, Wendy, Mike, Carol, Edna, Barbara, and Beverly became the interim board members who would also be on the application as incorporators. Their next meeting would be on February 28, and after that, they would solidify plans to draw up the application. Its submission lay on the not-so-distant horizon.

As Bonnie left her last Women's Association meeting and went out into the night where her Volkswagen Beetle waited to carry her home from a women's bank meeting one final time, she shed no tears. True, she had poured a lot of energy into this project, and she might not even get her $1,000 back. It had been nearly a year since she'd first met up with Carol and together they'd invited their friends and colleagues to explore the idea of a bank. She'd gone in eager to learn and share, but in the days leading up to her resignation, her feeling about the entire project had shifted.

In any group, it is normal to expect differences of opinion and to even anticipate some tension when a subject like money is concerned. Yet Bonnie couldn't justify sticking around any longer. She still craved a way to financially empower minority groups, though. Back before she'd moved to Denver as a divorcée and single mother, she had experienced financial discrimination when she found herself without credit and in need of a full tank of gas she couldn't pay for. She'd worked out a deal with the owner of the gas station she frequented: She would establish an account and pay it off each month for a year. At the end of that year, if she had paid everything off on time, she'd formally have credit there.

When she arrived in Denver ready to get her nursing degree, she'd also found it impossible to locate a realtor who was willing to take her to look at the new-home construction projects that were popping up everywhere in town and its outskirts. Instead of a modern new home, she'd had to settle for something older, taking over someone else's mortgage. She understood the need for a financial institution for women in Denver from personal experience. But she couldn't get behind the group if its main goal was to be a bank that was similar to others already in existence and that didn't serve her target demographic.

Bonnie was also frustrated with the way events had unfolded and the resulting inability to come to a consensus about the group's mission. It hadn't been that long ago that they were jovial and united in what was proposed. Being part of the project had been both exciting and pleasant for her. There had been invitations to come to others' homes, complete with hand-drawn maps in the minutes to help guide them. At one point, she had even hosted group members at her home for a potluck dinner, encouraging them to bring their best dishes, covering her table in Corelle bakeware.

She wouldn't let it get too bittersweet, though. Although she was no longer part of this group looking to start a women's bank, she still had work to do. Women still needed her. Bonnie Andrikopoulos was out of the group, but she was far from through.

CHAPTER 15

Wendy

Summer 1974

As is customary in the Wild West, there are heists. But, then, there are *heists*.

Standing outside Denver's Brown Palace Hotel with a few colleagues on this day in 1974, thirty-two-year-old Wendy Wittlin Davis was about to pull off a *heist*.

To the onlooker taking in the group outside the building, one of the most iconic in the city, Wendy and her colleagues might have looked like any other unassuming lunch bunch. But, like with many a former surprising Wild West outlaw, appearances can be deceiving. They were there on a mission. The practice of sex discrimination against women patrons in the Brown Palace's members-only club dining room was about to be outed. Now all that was left to do was go inside and raise the ruckus.

It had been two years since the Davis family had moved to the Denver area from Virginia and settled in the family-friendly neighborhood of Lakewood. Rather than work solely as a homemaker, Wendy found work as an attorney with the Denver Housing and Urban Development (HUD) office.

She had also gotten active with Denver's NOW chapter. It was there that she'd met Bonnie Andrikopoulos, and they had worked together on several grassroots campaigns, including stumping for the newly reintroduced ERA. Eventually, she would join Bonnie for the early meetings with Carol Green to discuss forming a bank. Bonnie, always working to put women in power, got Wendy appointed to the City of Lakewood Liquor Licensing Authority.

Wendy had grown up in the Buffalo-Niagara area of New York, which lies over three hundred miles away from New York City. Around the time she graduated from high school, Wendy hatched a financially savvy plan. When she learned that Cornell offered free tuition for home economics majors, she applied. To the modern-day reader, such a major might seem puzzling for someone who'd one day study law. Wendy, however, saw the major as an opportunity to take advantage of other courses offered by the Ivy League institution. The benefit being that, thanks to her major, those courses would also be free of charge for in-state students. In 1961, she married and transferred to Hunter College, where she completed her BS in home economics.

By 1964, Wendy was a college graduate, married, and a mother of one young child. Her small family moved to Ann Arbor, Michigan, to accommodate her husband, who was in residency at the University of Michigan after graduating from medical school. Wendy put her home ec degree to good use and secured a position as a dietitian in a University of Michigan dormitory. Then she got an idea that she simply couldn't shake: she wanted to attend law school. She applied and was accepted to study law at the prestigious University of Michigan.

Many women ended up following their husbands should a promotion or job take him elsewhere. Wendy differed, though, since few of those wives following their husbands were also studying for a law degree during such a transition. Life carried on, and Wendy adjusted to it and kept studying.

She adjusted and studied while raising their first child. She adjusted and studied after her husband secured a post in Virginia. And when the family moved south, she transferred to the College of William & Mary, where she also was associate editor of the *Law Review*.

In the American culture of the late 1960s, the establishment still wasn't required to accept or take female professionals seriously. Job titles and careers such as that of attorney were presumed to belong primarily to men. Women, if they worked outside the home, were expected to spend a handful of years working in fields that were considered more appropriately "feminine" in nature. The more widely accepted female roles were caretaking, raising children, and running the household. This is why so many educated women poured into fields like nursing, teaching, or social work.

After the requisite time spent working, they would presumably move on to the position of wife and mother. Women seeking degrees in law were a rare, bold sisterhood often subjected to reminders of the implications that accompanied their decision to pursue law. The dean at William & Mary was no exception and fully prepared to sound his alarm.

In an office meeting, he explained to Wendy, "If you take jobs after completing law school, your daughters will end up unwed and your sons will end up in prison."

Amused by him at best, Wendy finished up her law degree. During one of her final exams, Wendy was eight months pregnant with her second child. Her classmates left empty seats all around her. It was as if they were worried that she might explode or give birth right there during the exam. In the end, Wendy not only made it through the test, but she passed, graduated with her law degree, and gave birth to her second child. Several years later, Colorado beckoned and the family moved west.

The term "sexual discrimination" is commonplace now, thanks to modern-day activism and lawsuits. But on that fateful afternoon in the summer of 1974, when Wendy and four of her colleagues set out for their business lunch at Denver's Brown Palace Hotel, steak and potatoes weren't on the menu. Sexual discrimination, which was often carried on in plain view without being called out, was the lone item anyone in the group intended to dine on.

At over a century and a quarter old, the Brown Palace is one of several buildings among historic Denver's crown jewels. Even now, it is unmistakably frozen in time, with whimsical touches from that bygone Wild West era that also hearkens back to the adventures of railway travel. It is an ornate, Italian Renaissance–inspired, reddish-colored building made entirely of fireproof materials that include iron, steel, and concrete. Its exterior blends red Colorado granite with sandstone imported from nearby Arizona.

Taking in its finery and elegance, it is easy to overlook that the structure was first commissioned as an act of revenge and defiance by a local man named Henry C. Brown. Brown was a carpenter and entrepreneur who had traveled westward in 1860 from Ohio by oxcart. He had settled in the area near Cherry Creek and acquired 160 acres of land that would one day become much of metro Denver. His land portfolio included the triangular plot located at Broadway, Tremont, and Seventeenth Streets, where the Brown Palace still stands.

As his land increased in value, Brown shed very little of his down-home oxcart-driving ways. This was despite becoming a substantially wealthy landowner. He is credited with the construction of buildings and infrastructure that became part of Denver's first communities, some of which continue to withstand the test of time. Brown was known for being a generous man and unafraid to share his wealth. He donated the patch of land that became the site of the state capitol and gave $1,000 of his own money to help establish the region's first public library.

But no one is immune to awkward moments in life, even former pioneers turned wealthy landowners. One fateful afternoon, Brown came face-to-face with a bit of his destiny after the nearby Windsor Hotel refused him admission. The reason? He was dressed in what they considered to be "cowboy clothing," which wasn't permitted at the Windsor. Many people in town at that time, including Brown, owned cattle. To anyone with a lick of farm sensibility, tending to a herd of cattle or conducting farm chores in a suit and tie or wearing shiny church shoes was ludicrous and completely out of the question. Brown had the money to pay a meal bill, so why shouldn't he be allowed to dine there? Was it really just because of his clothing?

A furious Brown departed the Windsor and vowed to get even in a way that only the privileged few can. He enacted his revenge by creating a spectacular hotel that would become famous and that also bore his name. The Brown Palace aimed to outdo the Windsor in class and opulence, with one caveat. Patrons could still wear their "cowboy clothing" inside.

Brown designated the triangular plot, a spot where his cows often grazed, as the location to carry out his plans. They broke ground in 1888 and opened the hotel in 1892. All told, the Brown Palace cost $1.6 million to construct and another $400,000 to furnish. Brown's vision became a reality, and it gathered plenty of local interest for its modern elegance. At the time of its opening, the Brown Palace was the second fireproof building in the nation and the tallest building in Denver. It had four hundred guest rooms that rented out to travelers and guests for three to five dollars a night.

Long after Brown died, the hotel continued to honor his goals. Popular guests at the hotel have included most sitting US presidents since Teddy Roosevelt; Buffalo Bill Cody; The Beatles, who stayed there after a concert at nearby Red Rocks Park; and the "unsinkable" Molly Brown. Brown was not related to Henry C. Brown, but she stayed at the hotel often, including two weeks after she survived the tragic sinking of the *RMS Titanic*. She became a known and beloved guest for her courteous treatment of all staff whom she encountered.

Afternoon high tea is a Brown Palace staple. It is served daily in the atrium by staff educated in the ceremony and art of English tea service. Guests have a choice of sipping Brown's tea or Royal Palace tea as they listen to live music. The Brown Palace is one of the only locations in the West that provides a proper British tea service.

The hotel has also remained true to Brown's commitment to combine elegance with enthusiasm for western cowboy culture. Since 1945, one of its most celebrated and distinguished annual guests has been the top prizewinning steer from Denver's annual stock show. The winning steer, weighing anywhere from fifteen hundred to two thousand pounds, is brought straight into the regal hotel. It enjoys a cherished moment in the limelight, where it is displayed in the hotel's grand atrium lobby before being carted off to the slaughterhouse.

But unfortunately for the hotel in 1974, all that sheen and history couldn't change the fact that the staff was also still enforcing an archaic rule. They seemed unaware of the irony that a hotel built to rebut one kind of discrimination was now engaging in another. Although women were welcome to enjoy lunch at all of the hotel's other restaurants, they were not permitted to eat lunch in the club dining room. But on that fateful midmorning in late June 1974, when Wendy and her colleagues stepped inside for lunch, the laws had recently changed. Discrimination on the basis of sex in public accommodations like hotels and restaurants was now illegal. The group conducting the ambush that day consisted of two men and three women, all colleagues and attorneys with HUD. The dining room where they wanted to stage their protest had a members-only policy, and they needed an in. That in would be their colleague Jack Toll, who had the idea in the first place. He was planning to retire from his job and to resign from the club.

Now, as the fivesome arrived at the club, Jack Toll stood at the front of the line, asking the maître d' for a table for himself and his four guests. He was greeted as though he were a long-lost friend, one member of the group would recall.

But the smiles faded and the warm welcome started and ended with Toll. His guests were curtly reminded of the club's longtime policy.

"Ladies can't eat in here. Ladies aren't permitted!"

These frantic, firm words from the maître d' were exactly what they'd expected. They had set out to prove that the dining room would refuse service to women. And with those simple words, the maître d' had confirmed their suspicions.

The Brown Palace was discriminating.

They didn't get a seating that afternoon, but the group left the hotel with the ammunition they were seeking. It seemed that the Brown Palace wasn't yet ready to join the '70s. It was still clinging to an outdated tradition, and now they had the proof. It was time to file a lawsuit.

Forbidding women access to the same spaces as men was still a common practice in 1972 when Marc Fasteau wrote about the act of clubbiness and its impact in *Ms.* magazine. Men provided excuses that included having to stand up for women every time they entered the room, an inability to discuss sports, fear of women adding feminine touches such as green tablecloths, and the implication that they'd "destroy the club as 'a bastion to the madness of the outside world.'"

He wondered why when women participated it took away the power of drinking brandy and smoking cigars, and why the thought of having a woman in the National Security Council was so jarring.

He wrote that his guess was because "acting like a man" required toughness and control over themselves and those who depended on them—a tough expectation to live up to—men had developed coping mechanisms to affirm their masculinity, such as excluding women from "foreign policy and high finance."

High finance—or any finance, for that matter—was important to women. And whether readers agreed with Fasteau's key points, the incident in Denver at the Brown Palace shook the hotel to its core. That November, notice came to the group that the administration at the Brown Palace had relented. Through the hotel's spokesman and lawyer, they were told that "a policy to exclude women from the Brown Palace Club during the luncheon hour . . . has been terminated."

Wendy spoke to the *Denver Post* after the Brown Palace changed its policy. In a polka-dotted dress and wire-rimmed glasses, she expressed concern over the lack of professional respect women continued to receive. "It's demeaning to say that I, as a federal attorney, am not worthy to go to a business lunch where I want to!"

Lynn Brown, her colleague and a member of the original five, added, "Throughout, the hotel discriminated pleasantly. Yet it was infuriating to be told businessmen feel they can't do business if businesswomen are around! Men do business with businesswomen all the time in downtown Denver!"

Lunch was only one of many examples where the career woman could expect to meet that occasional brick wall reminding her that she was not exactly welcome in the space. But if Wendy Davis and her colleagues could make an establishment like the Brown Palace fall in line with the new laws, could she join forces with the Weight Watchers lady and others and successfully open a bank that gave women the banking service they deserved?

CHAPTER 16

The Charter

With memories of the rift still fresh and raw, the remaining members of the Women's Association continued to meet and finalize their charter application. It was a major milestone, the first step in being formally recognized as a legitimate entity intending to form a bank. Without an approved charter application, they couldn't do anything else on their checklist, like finalize a location and start renovation or start to sell stock. Because 1976 was a leap year, they had one extra day in February to let what had transpired fully sink in. They agreed that they wanted to adhere to the rules on the books, which meant strict enforcement of ownership stakes and other regulatory measures going forward.

Looking to the bank in New York City as a template of sorts, they could see that it was off to what appeared to be a pretty auspicious start, especially once naysayers like "Go Home!" Harry Britton had been pushed aside. It wouldn't become clear until after it had opened, when things should have been running smoothly, that the bank's finances remained precarious.

In March 1976, as the Women's Association in Denver was applying for their charter, the New York group reported that total deposits had grown from a daily average of $5.8 million in early December to $9.9 million earlier that month. However, they had also incurred net losses of $565,813 in the time period from incorporation to the end of 1975. That amount might have raised some eyebrows, but it wasn't enough to raise red flags.

One practical matter to address after the rift was the issue of members wanting to leave the group and to receive a full reimbursement of their $1,000 contributions. The events of February had taught them that the request for the money was no longer so simple. They had learned that, going forward, reimbursement would need to be voted on and that the vote needed to be a unanimous "no" so the project stayed solvent. They had budgeted based on the original number of members contributing $1,000 each. Now that Bonnie and the others had left the group, they were $4,000 short. If they were going to refund members who left, they would have to find the same number of new people to take their place.

The remedy for this potential exposure was fairly straightforward. Any new members, they agreed, would need a clear understanding that their $1,000 contribution was nonrefundable, even if they chose to leave. Going forward, it was also imperative for anyone with an interest in joining to understand both the philosophy and the mission of the now-official Women's Association. To avoid repeats like the rift, everyone who signed on would need to be on the same page. Supporting the idea of a bank was only half of the equation; they would also need to support the *plan* for bringing it to life.

The previous handful of meetings had taught them that when it came to serious bank business, there were protocols to consider. Group members could propose and debate things like locations or names for the bank as much as they liked. But once a charter application was filled out and signed, they were beholden to any and all applicable regulations and standards. The ownership issue that had caused the rift was a perfect example of this need put into practice. It was easy to look at what was happening in other banks within the sisterhood, like in New York, and to see their inability to fully sell their stock as a reason to allow for more ownership, but the rules would dictate otherwise.

With their names formally attached to the project, the incorporators had even more to consider. The project itself could have many founders. The Women's Bank would go on to woo fifty members who fell into that category alone, but incorporators had to be a distinct class within the leadership. Anyone who signed on as an incorporator had extra skin in the game. By law, the application process required each incorporator to study and successfully sit for an exam that would test their regulatory knowledge and their functional knowledge of how banks are properly run. Incorporators would be the names and faces of the proposed bank in the appeal to Colorado and then Washington, DC, for permission to organize. And they would put their personal information and their signatures on the line for the charter application. Becoming an incorporator was not a decision to be taken lightly.

Ten members agreed to be the official incorporators: Leslie Davis, Betty Freedman, Wendy Davis, Beverly Martinez-Grall, Loretta Norgren, Barbara Sudler, Mike Feinstein, Carol Green, Judi Foster, and Edna Mosley.

Like her fellow nine incorporators, Betty Freedman was ready to study for the exam and take it. Beyond the exam, each incorporator was required to complete what was called a biographical application and fill out a financial report disclosing their net worth. Honestly, though, Betty was fine with sharing this information.

Betty's application, neatly typed, relayed a brief synopsis of her life leading up to 1976 in snapshots. Here was her birth date and her education at Denver's East High School and then on to Goucher for college, where she'd met Marshall. Here, too, were her other last names, including Shapiro from when she had been married to her late first husband, Bob. She had also listed the different boards she sat on, including the Women's Library Association at the University of Denver and the Benefits Council for the Denver Art Museum. She'd bought one hundred shares of the proposed bank for a total of $1,000, and her references included the family rabbi, Earl Stone. When asked to list any children in the home, it's likely she reflected fondly on how time had flown. It hadn't been that long ago that she had sat in their rooms reading from the well-worn pages of their Dr. Seuss books while their eyelids blinked more and more slowly as they drifted off to sleep. Now Tracy was seventeen and a debutante, and Jon was away at college and practically a grown man. Dougie, forever suspended in time, would always be her baby. Her eternal, beautiful baby.

For the financial report, the Freedmans had gone digging into their files for the information they needed and then had listed out their assets and accounts. They'd invested in a handful of companies and held insurance policies. They also had a few bank accounts, including at Guaranty, where Betty knew and enjoyed the company of "Miss LaRae" Orullian when they had occasion to catch up.

The last item of business on both her forms and the group application was her signature, which she etched into the paper with delicate swoops in the "B," "S," and "F" of her name, Betty Sue Freedman.

As Betty had done, the other incorporators filled out the biographical and financial applications and revealed their lives and finances. Once all ten signatures had been added to the back pages, it was both finished and exciting. They had endured a long stretch of planning and preparing to get to this point. They had agreed on putting the word "women's" somewhere in the bank's name, and they had also agreed to propose setting up in the Equitable Building located at Seventeenth and Stout Streets. And now it was time to wait for word of approval from the comptroller.

And wait they would.

CHAPTER 17

Gail

Summer 1976

Waiting on word from the comptroller's office didn't mean that the Women's Association didn't have things to do. Although some tasks, like getting stock subscriptions and pledge deposits or renovating their space, would have to wait for charter approval, they could still plan ahead for what they would do after they received an update on their charter application. Several committees formed around steps that could be taken while they waited, including the newsletter, media, and marketing committees.

Beverly Martinez-Grall had been with the group since its beginnings in Carol Green's living room. She had been one of the handful of people who'd first attended a meeting at the behest of Bonnie Andrikopoulos, and after Bonnie's departure, she'd gotten more involved. She had sat through plenty of jovial meetings and also witnessed the rift, which inspired her to remind the group that if they were to be women for women, they'd need to present a unified front.

Born and raised in Denver, the capable, dark-haired beauty had worked her way up at channel 2. As the current host of the local interest show *Denver Now*, Beverly was a recognizable face. *Denver Now* explored social issues, even taking time to visit a local prison to speak in depth with inmates. Working toward opening a bank that would serve women and other minority populations was right up her street.

Although many committees were forming, media outreach was a natural fit. The Women's Association would need a media strategy if the charter was approved, and a different one if it was rejected. After years at channel 2, Beverly also had many contacts in Denver media circles.

One newcomer that spring was also ready to hit the ground running. Her name was Gail Schoettler. She joined several committees, including the newsletter, the planning, and the building committees. She would eventually be elected to the board. That she would one day join the Women's Association and work shoulder to shoulder to organize the Women's Bank could almost be called part of her destiny. Gail had been in leadership positions since high school and had participated in groups and demonstrations in college that pushed for more equality.

Gail balanced a life that included the roles of wife and mother, her work with the Children's Museum of Denver, and studies for a PhD in African history. Gail and Judi lived in the same neighborhood, but they met quite by accident. One fated day, their husbands were walking the family dogs, and the pets got into a row. During the tussle, Judi's dog ripped Gail's dog's ear. A few days later, the doorbell rang at the Schoettler home, and there stood Judi with a bouquet of apology flowers in hand. Unlike their dogs, the pair hit it off almost instantly and became fast friends.

Gail and Judi had been born just one month apart, and like Judi, Gail had grown up in the world of California agriculture. Instead of growing fruit trees, her family ran a cattle ranch. She learned early on that if a boy could do something, so could she. The Sintons raised Gail and her twin sister, Patricia, to see that nothing around the ranch was off limits, and no task was too difficult. They would assist during the birthing of baby calves. They swung hammers and pounded nails to maintain fences. They helped with branding and vaccinating the cattle.

Both of the girls' parents had attended college, their father at Berkeley and their mother at UCLA, and the expectation was that Gail and Patricia would do the same.

Gail's non-ranch-related education took place at the tiny town school. She and the same seventeen classmates kept after one another, starting in the first grade through their senior year of high school. During high school, five teachers juggled seven periods and six classrooms. Student clubs included Future Homemakers of America (FHA) for the girls and Future Farmers of America for the boys.

Gail became a leader in the FHA, first at the community level and then the state level. A teacher who spotted her potential encouraged her to run for president of the California chapter.

She did, and she won. At the 1959 convention, Gail delivered a speech, titled "Your Responsibilities as Future Homemakers of America," to more than nine thousand of her fellow FHA participants.

In the fall of 1960, Gail entered college with the freshman class at Stanford, originally intending to study chemistry. But a lack of foundational courses from high school caused her to switch out of the major. During a study-abroad program at Stanford's Florence, Italy, campus in 1962 and early 1963, an econ professor persuaded the striking, confident, tanned rancher's daughter with dark hair and sparkly brown eyes to major in economics. She became one of just three female students in the major that year.

In April 1964, Gail had waited in line with her fellow classmates for several hours to hear Dr. Martin Luther King Jr. speak about the civil rights movement. Energized by the change taking hold, Gail took action on more-personal issues as well. Stanford had long upheld certain standards and rules. During Gail's time at Stanford, these standards and rules included protocols that applied in specific places on campus where she and her fellow female students were not allowed to wear pants. Stanford also enforced a set of rules known as "the social rules." When Gail was a student, under the social rules, a female student would be issued a demerit if she was out so much as a minute past curfew. Enough demerits and she could find herself in serious hot water.

It didn't matter if the female student in question had been studying at the library or out on a date. What was most important to Gail and her dorm mates was that they were being held to a standard that their fellow male students weren't. Male students were not subject to a curfew or demerits for being out too late. The only thing to do was lobby for the social rules to be relaxed and for the curfew to be abolished.

If she could copyedit the school's paper of record and participate in important activism events right alongside her male peers, she and her fellow female students should be able to stay out past arbitrary curfews without fear of outdated retribution, they'd reasoned. Together they fought for and ultimately won more-relaxed rules, changing the circumstances not only for themselves but for every coed who came after them.

Now, as part of the Women's Association, Gail was ready to help fight a different sort of battle on behalf of women—the battle for funds. If the group was granted a charter, there would be a great deal of money to raise in the form of both stock purchases and deposit pledges. Stock purchases are direct shares of the bank, while deposit pledges are a promise of sorts given by the depositor to put a certain amount into an account. Both call on the general public to participate, with one caveat: a stock purchase comes with no guarantees. In addition to being part of the group's newsletter committee, Gail signed on to be part of the team that would go out and raise awareness about the proposed Women's Bank. With her background in economics, she was uniquely suited to explain stock purchases and deposit pledges to the general public. And hopefully, by building that awareness, she could also help the group raise enough money to organize and operate a successful bank.

CHAPTER 18

Mary Roebling

July 1976

After the excitement of filing the charter application in March, the ennui of waiting set in. April brought sweet spring air and no update about the application. In May, with bicentennial buzz in the air along with the bumblebees looking for their nectar, no news came. June brought the expected stream of weddings and graduations without any news about the application. The Women's Association needed some good news, and July would *finally* bring them that, sort of. Although July didn't bring a firm update on their application, it did bring them Mrs. Mary Roebling.

On the Fourth, New York City's harbor filled with boats and its sky with fireworks as the two hundredth birthday of the USA kicked off. You couldn't go far that summer without seeing something to remind you of the nation's birthday, whether it was a souvenir coin to commemorate it or the New York City skyline alight with rockets.

As expected, a dry, sunshine-drenched heat swept into Denver that summer, and local headlines decried the effects of air pollution and smog.

For the Women's Association, it was still important to think ahead. There were many things that needed to be done after they received charter approval and before they could then file for approval to open. However, without knowing the fate of their charter application, their hands were tied when it came to crucial steps like selling stock and renovating their space.

When the group had applied for the charter in March, they had tentatively forecasted an approval that placed sometime in 1977 as their potential target date to open for business. In the interim, they had busied themselves with those few things they could accomplish while they waited. Minutes from that summer and fall reveal how they couldn't conduct much new business because they were still waiting.

Stock subscriptions, for instance, which were a large part of the bank's formation, could not proceed until after the group's petition for a charter was approved. Although Gail Schoettler and her team couldn't yet sell the stock, they could still get ready to sell it by soliciting interest in the project, but that was all they could do. The silence coming from the comptroller no doubt gave some pause, but there was plenty to do to keep busy. In the spring, the group discussed one dilemma they could fix: they needed a respected financial mentor to help them be taken seriously. This person would have to be a woman.

Over notes and coffee and amid the occasional puff of cigarette smoke, they wondered aloud who this mentor might be. They had seen how essential the mentorship of Madeline McWhinney and Betty Friedan had been to the now-open First Women's Bank in New York City. But who could fill that role in Denver?

No one remembers exactly when the *Business Week* article on the top women in business began to make the rounds at meetings, but everyone had read it. The executive search committee, composed of long-standing members, including Betty and Carol, decided it might be a good idea for the group to reach out to the few women in banking mentioned in the article. Madeline McWhinney was one woman featured in the article. Like Betty, she was a Denver native and socialite whose comings and goings had been announced in the papers as a child. She was also respected in banking and economic circles and was prominently featured in the press while gearing up to be the inaugural leader of the New York City bank. Carol Green had spoken with her on several occasions over the past few months, and she had agreed to advise them for a fee, but they had yet to fully take her up on the offer.

In addition to Madeline McWhinney's, there were eight other names in the article to consider. Eight possibilities for a yes. The executive search committee discussed the matter of who would write these women letters of introduction. All of the women were based in big cities, mostly on the coasts. Who could speak their language and best represent the women of Cow Town?

"I'll do it."

Wendy Davis looked up from her reading. The voice belonged to Betty Freedman, the socialite and fundraiser. As one of Denver's foremost movers and shakers, she was the perfect candidate.

"I can send letters to each woman," she said. "I'll introduce our association and let them know what we're doing out here."

Appeal to their knowledge and skill, one attendee had mused.

Ask if they'll come to Denver to be part of our project.

Tell them you saw them in the article too.

Betty nodded, her pen flying across her notepad. Obviously, this introduction would include the standard stuff, even if the subject of the letters was somewhat unconventional.

Wendy, who'd always respected Betty's contributions, admired her in this instant for her chutzpah. It took bravery to appeal to the upper-echelon women in finance and banking, as she'd be doing. Writing them out of the blue and asking for some help was gutsy. Since the *BusinessWeek* article had been published, surely there were a myriad of letter writers just like herself filling up the mailboxes of these women. They were a long shot.

Several days later, Betty took the article and mailing addresses, sat down at her desk, and wrote an introductory letter to each of the women on the list. It was easy to wonder who might reply. Hopefully with a bit of gusto and real interest in helping them out.

Would it be Catherine B. Cleary, president and chief executive officer of First Wisconsin Trust Company, Milwaukee, with deposits of $20.8 million? The only woman to head a well-known bank she had not inherited, according to the article.

Or maybe Rebecca S. High, senior vice president of First Pennsylvania Bank, Philadelphia. She also seemed promising. Philadelphia was known as the "city of brotherly love," but could there also be some sisterly banking in the cards? And could it extend itself all the way to Denver? That year, First Pennsylvania was ranked the nineteenth-largest bank in the nation, with deposits of $4.4 billion.

Not to be overlooked was Marilyn LaMarche, vice president at Citibank, New York City, listed as the country's second-largest bank, with deposits of $45 billion. "As head of the business development department of the personal financial management division, LaMarche handles portfolios totaling more than $100 million," read the article.

Notably, however, none of the women in the article ran a bank that lay west of the Mississippi, or within even one hundred miles of Cow Town. It was high time to push from the nation's mind a few of the images of wild cowboys or a lack of culture that often went hand in hand with the Wild West label attached to places such as Denver. It was time to show there was a more serious, moneyed side of this Cow Town.

Starting with the first name, Betty's determined, manicured hands flew as she wrote letters that might have read something like this:

> Dear Ms. Cleary:
> I am Mrs. Freedman from Denver, Colorado. I read about you in *BusinessWeek* magazine. A few of us are wanting to explore the possibility of opening a bank here for women. I have contacted you to see if you might have an interest in meeting with us.
> Gratefully Yours,

Mrs. Marshall Freedman
Denver, Colorado

One by one, the envelopes piled up. Betty kept going until the letters were written: Catherine B. Cleary in Milwaukee; Rebecca S. High in Philadelphia; Marilyn LaMarche in New York City; Kay K. Mazuy in Boston; Sandra J. McLaughlin in Pittsburgh; Caroline Norman in Winston-Salem, North Carolina; Martha R. Seger in Detroit; and last but not least, Mary Roebling in Trenton, New Jersey. When she was satisfied with her work, Betty stamped each envelope and rose to deposit them in the mailbox. Work completed, she could report back that the outreach was done. Now all they had to do was wait to hear back.

Waiting on responses to the outreach letters. Waiting on an update from the comptroller's office. Who knew opening a bank involved so much waiting?

By the time Betty's envelope arrived at the desk of Mary Gindhart Herbert Roebling in Trenton, the surname Roebling was well known and respected in many social and political circles. At seventy-one, Mary was a formidable woman and could only be described as utterly unforgettable. A respected executive, she was a stylish, whip-smart, powerful yet feminine force within the financial industry.

Mrs. Roebling hadn't always been the towering, smartly dressed financial icon that the group in Denver hoped might entertain the idea of helping them. But through her force of will, hard work, and perhaps even a bit of kismet, she was now a powerhouse with a proven record of striking gold in matters of business and finance. And striking gold is what Denver was all about.

Born in West Collingswood, New Jersey, in 1905 to Isaac, a phone-company executive, and Mary Simon Gindhart, a music teacher, Mary was the eldest of four children. Like LaRae Orullian, she took on her first "career" at a young age working as a fruit picker, selling boxes of freshly picked strawberries for a penny apiece. She attended the local public schools and, at one time, had expressed interest in becoming an actress. She didn't complete high school but, instead, married Arthur Herbert, a World War I veteran and a musician, when she was seventeen. Two years later, Arthur died suddenly of blood poisoning, leaving Mary not only widowed at the tender age of nineteen but also with the task of raising their young daughter, Elizabeth.

She returned home with her daughter to be closer to family, but she didn't languish there long. She was prepared to provide a life for the two of them despite the obstacles. At twenty-one years old, she wasn't exactly a spinster. Still, any widow with a child could expect difficulties getting back out there on the dating scene. Mary appeared to shelve the idea of romance when she moved to Philadelphia, taking work as a salesgirl at Blum's department store during the day. At night, she attended classes in merchandising and business administration at the University of Pennsylvania's Wharton School. At the time, legend has it, women were discouraged from taking classes during the daytime hours.

Eventually, Mary quit her department store job after finding work as a secretary at a local brokerage firm. But the nuances of department stores and what they represented to women, on both the personal and consumer levels, were never far from Mary's mind. She'd done well for herself and moved up the ladder to the role of customer consultant. While she was working at the brokerage firm, she met wealthy, handsome Siegfried Roebling. In that moment, her life took a dramatic turn. Mary, who came from a financially comfortable background, could link her family back to William the Conqueror. Yet she was outdone in spades by Siegfried Roebling.

Like the Carnegies, whose name was synonymous with steel, or the Rockefellers with oil, the Roebling family had made their industrial age fame and fortune through wire rope and cable. John Roebling, Siegfried's great-grandfather, started the company as a wire-rope business in Saxonburg, Pennsylvania.

Roebling was the family that bridged some of the most notable patches of land that were once separated by water and could only be crossed by boat. The nation's best-known suspension bridges, including the Golden Gate in San Francisco and the George Washington in New York City, were cabled by Roebling. But the Brooklyn Bridge is the most significant structure linked to the name Roebling. Siegfried's great-grandfather John designed the bridge, which was considered a modern marvel and ahead of its time. Although he was a big part of the story, he would not get to see his project reach completion. Before the structure was even partially constructed, John perished in an accident.

Colonel Washington A. Roebling, John's son, then assumed operations, determined to see his father's vision to completion. The family endured another disaster on the project after he suffered from decompression sickness at the worksite, which left him disabled. With two men down for the count, a woman in the Roebling family stepped up. Washington's wife, Emily, took over as the third overseer of the project. Emily had better luck than John and Washington and was able to see the bridge built to completion. In 1883, Emily Roebling possibly pressed her luck but was the first human to cross the finished bridge that connected Manhattan to Brooklyn.

When the colonel's grandson Siegfried met young, widowed Mary Herbert, he was working as vice president of the family company, John A. Roebling's Sons. He was taken by the gorgeous former shopgirl with a great mind for business and the pedigreed education to back it. The pair eventually married and added a son, Paul, to the family. Because Siegfried Roebling had plenty of money, Mary, who had worked for the better part of her adult life, now planned to stay home to raise the children.

On January 2, 1936, Mary awoke in Los Angeles, California, in a room at the Biltmore Hotel that she shared with Siegfried. They'd just come west a few days prior to celebrate the New Year and attend a football game. Something was wrong with Siegfried, who was still and lifeless. After doctors sped to the scene, they would pronounce him dead, citing cardiac arrest as the culprit. His death meant that Mary was now a widow twice over.

This time, however, materially speaking, the family would be better taken care of. Mary had work experience and her college courses. Even in the direst of financial circumstances, she still probably wouldn't have had to find work in a department store this time around. Her education and experience wouldn't be her necessary fallbacks either. Siegfried had willed his substantial estate to their son, Paul, who was a toddler at the time, making Mary the trustee.

Part of Siegfried's holdings in the Roeblings' company included a majority ownership of the local Trenton Trust. With the nation in the thick of the Great Depression, the bank had been deemed insolvent. Desperate for answers about what to do with the bank, Mary had appealed to both her father and father-in-law for advice.

Mary, they had said to her, the bank is in such bad shape that you should go in and run it, because you can't do any worse.

Can't do any worse?

Mary pondered those words for a bit. But it wasn't that advice that stuck with her. Both men had also reminded her that she had what made a bank thrive. She had common sense.

Realizing she'd inherited "an opportunity and nothing more," she decided to take her chances on the flailing bank. On January 21, 1937, thirty-one-year-old Mary Roebling became president of the Trenton Trust. Mrs. Roebling was revered, from her hairstyles to her business acumen. If the press loved the smart socialite from the instant she sat at her desk before a row of awaiting press cameras to officially sign her first swath of documents, then the public adored her.

Some banks had a long-standing reputation for being unwelcoming, stodgy institutions where insiders thrived and outsiders stumbled. Mrs. Roebling decided that certainly wouldn't do on her watch. Now that she was in charge, one of the first changes she implemented was to literally tear down the imposing walls that for generations had siloed banking's upper management from the public. She wanted her bank to be accessible, approachable, and a place that people enjoyed visiting. Declaring that banks were the "department stores of finance," she emphasized top-notch, customized service. She also enjoyed redecorating the main bank building with whimsical themes, similar to what a window-shopper might gaze on as they peered dreamily into the windows at their local downtown department store.

Mrs. Roebling's friendlier approach to banking also included intentional catering to the bank's women clients. She was an outspoken advocate of equal pay for women and established a women's division. At Trenton Trust, she also offered special services aimed toward women's clubs and groups.

When she took over the bank in 1937, the Trenton Trust had a reported $17 million in assets, which grew to a reported $210 million in assets by 1972. Mrs. Roebling served as a model iconoclast, dotting both the society and business pages of magazines and newspapers.

"Probably the only feminine president of a major bank and undoubtedly the best looking one," wrote the *Sarasota Herald*, adding that she was "tall, slender and addicted to gay beach pajamas."

She was frequently included in lists of the top ten richest women in the country, once to her chagrin, when a trio of bandits raided her suite, making off with nearly $500,000 in jewels and furs; when caught, they confessed that they knew the place was well stocked because they'd learned about it courtesy of a recent interview she had done.

By the mid-1950s, Mrs. Roebling was as likely to make headlines for her fashion sense as she was for counseling women on how to run a profitable business. She always had advice for female executives and hopefuls about navigating the male-dominated world of finance. In one article, the dilemma centered on dining out. Traditionally, bank presidents were men, and they picked up the tab. As a female bank president, she was anything but typical. Her position presented a problem of sorts because men weren't always keen to let a woman pay their bill. To solve her conundrum, she got creative and made arrangements with her favorite places. They agreed to never present the table with a check.

Instead, they would sign her name to the bill, add a tip, and then mail her the tab. This was just a small example of how Mary Roebling blazed her own trail without ruffling too many feathers. She knew that if she ruffled male feathers over every little thing, she'd never get anything done, so she smoothed egos where she could and chose her battles. She used it to her advantage that most businessmen had never dealt with a woman like her. But having achieved success, she didn't want to keep her methods to herself. Mary Roebling believed in helping those who came after her, which was lucky for the Denver Women's Association.

CHAPTER 19

You Girls

Betty could barely wait until she got back into the house to read her letter from Mrs. Roebling. She tore open the envelope, and her blue eyes scanned the words. Betty nearly jumped for joy. It seemed the idea of a bank for women in the Wild West had indeed piqued her interest. Mrs. Roebling had explained in the letter that she was headed to California soon and would be happy to detour to Denver on her way out. Would July 23 and 24 work for the group? Nobody would admit a group readiness to move heaven and earth to make it happen, but they could coolly respond that, yes, it certainly would work. Two whole days together? Betty could hardly wait until the next Women's Association meeting to discuss the good news. She had calls to make. Planning for Mrs. Roebling's visit must begin immediately.

It was Betty who had driven her family's compact car out to Stapleton Airport to pick up Mrs. Roebling. Betty had also gotten to know Mrs. Roebling a little on their drive to the only logical place in town to put up someone of her stature when they visited, the Brown Palace Hotel.

A few things were going to be different about the meeting that would take place when they hosted Mrs. Roebling on the twenty-fourth. It wasn't just the buzzy, excited feeling in the air either. They had done some behind-the-scenes scrambling to make this meeting a more formal one. Rather than in someone's living room or the conference room at an office, this particular meeting would take place at The Inverness, a local hotel and golf club. And in addition to Mary Roebling, there would be another special guest in attendance on that hot summer day, a man named Paul Howes.

At forty-six, Paul Howes was slightly balding, with bright eyes and a friendly smile. Importantly, he was a widely respected professional in the banking field. His career included setup work, like when he helped to put together the Wyoming Bancorporation. Howes understood western banking and its culture well, and like Judi Foster, he was connected and well plugged into the local networks. Howes lived in nearby Colorado Springs, and together with Mrs. Roebling, he was there to advise at the meeting.

After welcoming their esteemed guests, Judi had news all around. Frank Vick, one of their lawyers, had written to update her on the status of their charter application. For one sweet moment, there was excitement in the room and hope for a great update. But it wasn't exactly good news. After weeks of radio silence from the comptroller's office, Vick had finally learned that their charter application was still sitting, unread and unapproved, in Denver. It had been there now for four months and counting.

All was not lost, though. Frank Vick had also managed to pry a promise from the assistant comptroller that the application would leave Denver for Washington, DC, no later than August 6. Amid the grumbling, Mike Feinstein shook his head. He was one of the few men who had been part of the project from the beginning. He also knew firsthand that they had taken great pains to make sure their application was properly filled out.

He voiced a question many at the meeting were thinking: "Is this intentional?"

A few heads bobbed up and down. Nearly every woman in the room harbored the same suspicion as Mike. After all, if they had done the requested legwork—and they had—what other reasons might there be for a delay? How could the authorities not have so much as glanced at their application after all this time?

In a warm, reassuring tone, Mrs. Roebling asked, "May I respond?"

Of course she could. Every single soul in that room wanted to know what Mary Roebling thought about why their application was jammed up and still languishing in Denver.

Mrs. Roebling leaned forward, naturally commanding the room, and everyone listened. "It's possible that other Denver banks have said there are enough small banks in the area, that is one thing," she said. "The two recent bank failures out here would back that up."

The two recent bank failures were Skyline Bank and Coronado Bank. Their sagas and ultimate demises were big stories that had played out in the local news in Denver. As banks that had set out to serve a niche slice of the underbanked local population, their stories had been followed at Women's Association meetings, and the group had explored how to distinguish and even distance themselves from them. In knowing of Coronado and Skyline, too, it was clear to everyone in the room that Mary Roebling had done her homework about Denver before joining this meeting. If any doubts about whether she might take them seriously lingered, her A-plus knowledge about what was going on in Denver finance must have quelled some of those worries.

"But I would stress that a three-to-four-month delay is normal," she continued. That bit of news must have helped to reassure the group. "I also believe that the letter Paul Howes recently sent to the regional administrator will make a big difference."

This information from Mrs. Roebling helped the group feel more confident and worry less that they had sent their request into an unresponsive void. It also led them to reset their timeline. It now made more sense to assume that charter approval might arrive in November. Hypothetically, if a November approval came on the fifteenth—coincidentally, two days after Carol Green's birthday—they could then line up and execute a checklist and timeline that would prepare them for a June 1977 opening.

Later in the meeting, the stock-subscription committee reported that an estimated 60 percent of the bank's capitalization could be accomplished in six weeks. Mrs. Roebling nodded. "I would suggest that legal counsel provide you with the phrases to solicit stock-purchase commitments from responsible purchasers," she said. "Anywhere from ten to twenty women on the phones would be good for that task."

Paul Howes chimed in. "I feel that every share of stock should be in the hands of those who can help the bank, someone who would do business with the bank." There were many nods on this advice. Paul's was a good reminder that it wasn't just selling the stock but to *whom* it was sold that mattered, since stockholders would also have a say in how things were run.

As the formal meeting wound down, it was notable that everything Mrs. Roebling and Paul Howes had said was either something constructive or encouraging. It was reassuring to hear outside voices reinforce their optimism about the project. For Howes, western banking was a familiar thing, but it wasn't as directly familiar to Mrs. Roebling. Yet both guests were in favor of their project.

"That concludes our agenda," said Judi, turning to Mrs. Roebling and Paul Howes. "But I'd like to ask if you would both do us the honor of informally addressing our group and answering any questions we might have."

Mrs. Roebling nodded and looked directly at Judi. "You handled this meeting superbly," she said. Such a compliment from a legend like Mary Roebling was both flattering and encouraging. Judi smiled, hoping the heat in her cheeks wasn't causing too much of a noticeable blush.

"I also think you are fortunate to have Mr. Howes's support," Mrs. Roebling continued. "You must give him your unanimous support."

Supporting Paul Howes wouldn't be an issue; the group had already agreed that it would be a good idea to invite him to sign on to the project as a financial consultant. In turn, Howes had already thrown his considerable weight behind the project. In a letter to Kent Glover, regional administrator of national banks, dated July 8, 1976, he had appealed on behalf of the Women's Association as he wrote that he believed downtown Denver needed a bank "catering to the professional and working women," because he had witnessed discrimination against women by the existing banks. His analysis of the proposal for the bank found it "organized" and the feasibility study's findings were "highly conservative."

Mrs. Roebling, too, supported the group and continued her candid commentary. Like Paul Howes, she had examined their much-discussed feasibility study, finding it well done and worth the cost. "You seem to have things pretty well in hand," she said. Hearing this must have been a huge relief and provided encouragement to the members of the Women's Association who'd been tired of the waiting and wondering if they'd ever get this project off the ground.

The meeting wasn't without its cautionary moments, though. Mrs. Roebling also had her concerns about customer convenience. Specifically, given its location, they needed to consider availability of parking and the possibility of setting up drive-through facilities.

"I find the nationwide statistics revealing that drive-up and parking facilities are necessary," she advised. "Do you lack control on the depositor who has to go two or three blocks? For, you know, loyalty ends when it's a matter of convenience and money."

Still, convenience and what services to specifically offer wouldn't matter in the end if their charter application never got out of Denver with a stamp of approval. When the matter of the four-month delay came up, Mrs. Roebling offered her calm, reassuring advice again.

"Don't be discouraged about the application's holdup," she said. And then, in a gesture of solidarity that only a den mother such as her could possess, she smiled warmly. "I honestly believe you girls will be successful."

You girls.

Mrs. Roebling and Mrs. Roebling alone could get away with calling a roomful of successful, professional adult women "you girls." Had the term come from anyone else, there'd be questions. It seems that even Mike Feinstein was on board to be part of the "you girls" group without protest or clarification.

Mrs. Roebling's words of encouragement continued to fall over the group like a calming salve. They were tired of wondering about what their charter application being held up might mean. Without any concrete answers up to now, all that they could do was speculate. When a mind wanders, it will often skew toward extremes or negatives, but with Mrs. Roebling's knowledge and sage advice, they could all rest a little easier, assured that things would be moving along soon.

"You need to stand behind management fully and stay loyal to that management to ensure success," Mrs. Roebling also advised. "Women in the past haven't been loyal to other women, which has been the great fault of women."

Mrs. Roebling's advice about loyalty would be relatable to anyone who had been with the Women's Association since early 1976, when the rift between Carol Green and Bonnie Andrikopoulos threatened to derail the whole project.

Both Paul Howes and Mary Roebling gave advice on hiring top management. Howes was particularly concerned about the roles of president, executive vice president (EVP), and loan officer, since not many women who had the necessary experience and background worked in Denver. It wasn't impossible, but they'd be choosing from a small pool of applicants here. They had vetted the names of several prospects in past meetings, and while the pickings were not exactly slim, eligible women in banking had proved to be rare. Howes recommended that the presidency be held by a woman, but the EVP could be a man. Mrs. Roebling agreed, adding that "a couple of men seem to be necessary."

This comment got a few chuckles.

As the meeting wrapped, Mrs. Roebling made the group a unique promise about getting fully involved: "I'll have to talk this over with my astrologer, but I'll let you girls know."

You girls.

Coming from Mrs. Roebling, it always and forever felt like a compliment.

CHAPTER 20

Others Have Failed

As 1976 faded into 1977, the hoped-for deadline for charter approval came and went without word from the comptroller's office in Washington, DC. In a memo to the group, dated February 17, 1977, Judi wrote: "At this time, there appears to be no pressing need to hold a regular meeting in March as there is little business to transact until we hear from Washington. Therefore, the March 12 meeting is CANCELLED. Of course, if anything happens in the interim, you will be notified and an emergency meeting will be scheduled."

It would have been understandable if members of the Women's Association had been discouraged at this point in the process, but they vowed to keep themselves busy. The application might be in flux, but they could still take some comfort in the strides they had made. They had evolved from an informal group exploring the mere possibility of forming a women's bank into a formal organization awaiting government approval for a national charter. They'd garnered interest and support from serious backers both within and outside Colorado.

They also decided that the only way to really get the answers they sought was to take to the skies. The Women's Association was sending a few delegates to Washington, DC, to stump for them. In the same February 1977 memo, Judi reminded members of their homework ahead of the delegation's trip. "We need your help on LETTERS TO THE COMPTROLLER!!!" They hoped to have one hundred letters to send to Washington to add to their application, and Judi, usually quite calm, with her all caps and no fewer than three exclamation points in this memo, wanted to make sure everyone knew just how important these letters were. The memo detailed possible sample letters, including this one:

> I would like to express my interest in seeing that a charter be granted to the women of Denver who desire to bring to this community the Women's Bank. I feel that the Women's Bank concept can open doors to women who may be timid about talking about finances, loans for new businesses, for homes, etc. It will serve as an educational support system to the community, helping all financial institutions to grow with the women's growth. I hope that you will seriously consider granting this charter with the advantages it can offer.

The committees, from Edna's affirmative action to Gail's stock subscription, were now running efficiently as their own entities and continued to meet as needed. After giving up the top leadership position in the wake of the split, Carol Green had been appointed to run the marketing committee. This committee had worked on several outreach projects, including attending a fair that past summer named Woman '76, to learn if there might be interest among attendees in doing business with a women's bank. They came away with positive feedback. Betty Freedman ran the executive search committee and helped to solicit and vet potential candidates to run the bank once charter permission had been granted. These talented, connected members had also gone through their Rolodexes and pulled in relevant colleagues and contacts to assist in their efforts. With the help of Judi Foster and Paul Howes and the backing and support of Mary Roebling, the association pressed forward with optimism.

Allegedly, one culprit behind the application's delay was the recent closure of a local bank called Coronado Bank.

Coronado and Skyline were the names of two recently failed banks that had become quite familiar to the group. Both banks had been started with good intentions and aimed to serve Denver's underbanked and minority populations. They had both opened with great hope to be financial pillars for the communities they sought to serve, but both banks had fallen short and succumbed to difficult circumstances.

Skyline Bank had come along first. Introduced in 1970 as a multiracial institution, it was billed as the only bank of its kind in a downtown business district. Skyline drew from a diverse talent pool to form its organizers, directors, and staff. Organizers included heavy hitters like Jerome C. Rose, a local politician, and Dana Crawford, who made her name heading up Larimer Square Associates, a downtown Denver restoration and preservation organization.

Part of Skyline's plan was to occupy the iconic, historic Daniels and Fisher Tower. The building was now a stand-alone structure after the department store that it was once attached to, lovingly called "D&F," had been razed. Under the agreement, Skyline Tower, Inc., would work with a building company to incorporate the existing tower and build a new complex around it. In doing so, it would also restore the space to a modernized take on its former glory.

At the helm of the ambitious bank stood Lewis L. Gaiter Jr., an African American man who came from a banking background. He had served as a national bank examiner for the four years that led up to him getting involved with Skyline. His résumé also included a law degree from the University of Denver, work as a governor with the Metro Denver Fair Housing Center, and a seat on the board at the central YMCA. Gaiter also had practical, everyday banking experience that stretched back to 1966, when he'd worked at Denver's US National Bank.

When Skyline applied for its charter, it was the first bank in eight years in the downtown Denver area to apply for a national rather than a state charter. Skyline reported initial capitalization of $700,000, with $300,000 in capital, $100,000 in surplus, and $300,000 in undivided profit. The bank's location, at Seventeenth and Arapahoe Streets, put it squarely downtown and also made it a part of the famed financial district.

Skyline also went with an initial public offering. Its organizers made 40 percent of the bank's stock available to the public for purchase, representing 35,000 shares at $20 a share, for a grand total of $700,000. The public, in turn, had the option to buy anywhere from 5 to 350 shares of Skyline stock. These shares were made available to buyers who weren't in the organizing group or members of Skyline's board. They began to sell Skyline stock in April 1971, and by September 1971, Gaiter reported that roughly 75 percent of the stock had sold. Skyline's feasibility study projected that deposits would grow, starting with $3.5 million in deposits in the first year, $5 million in the second, and $8 million in the third.

It began with so much hope, yet by March 1973, local news headlines about Skyline told a difficult story and began to signal that a grim reckoning might be coming. In December 1972, after an examiner conducted a routine review of the bank, Skyline's issues were uncovered. Primarily, it had a low-liquidity problem coupled with an alarming exposure to loan losses. After the bank's liquidity dipped even lower, Skyline could only meet its financial obligations by raising money through an asset sale. On March 20, the bank sold off its loans to another financial institution to try and meet a $335,000 cash letter.

The sale was of little consequence. Skyline continued to slip further into the red.

By March 28, 1973, the comptroller's office stepped in, declaring Skyline insolvent, and changed the locks on the bank's doors. A day later, local headlines declared that United Banks of Colorado had put in an offer to buy Skyline for $802,000. Two additional banks had also bid for the institution. Aurora National Bank put in a much lower offer of $151,000, and Westland Banks in nearby Lakewood offered $425,000 for Skyline.

United Banks won out, and Skyline was renamed United Bank of Skyline, but the bank was far from being saved and able to reopen. A new charter had to be granted by the comptroller, and the acquisition required approval within thirty days by the board of governors of the Federal Reserve System. United Banks also had to agree to take over Skyline's assets and to make good on its deposits. To complete this bit of housekeeping, the FDIC steps in and subsidizes the difference between any assets and deposit payments. The acquirer then determines which of the loans it will keep and which it will discard.

Speaking to the press in the aftermath, Gaiter reported that he felt stunned about what had transpired at Skyline. The bank had begun with the best of intentions to finance the proverbial "little guy" and to preserve a treasured local landmark. But it had barely gotten off the ground before the deafening thud of its crash.

Perhaps one silver lining was the gentle attitude of United Banks toward the purchase of Skyline. United expressed its plans to offer former Skyline employees their same jobs at the new bank. Gaiter was asked to consider staying on, and United also agreed to honor the multiracial concept that had been a founding pillar at Skyline. Importantly, the cleanup of Skyline's financials meant that while depositors would probably not lose money, its shareholders might lose everything they had paid into it.

The rescue of Skyline was no fairy tale. Although slightly scathed, it had come out of going bust and steadied itself as best as it could. Coronado Bank, another minority bank in Denver, didn't fare as well.

Coronado was the vision of Francisco "Paco" Sanchez, a former state representative and the owner of KFSC, a local Spanish-language radio station. Coronado made local headlines around the same time as Skyline but for different reasons. In March 1973, Coronado opened its doors as a bank that would cater specifically to the local population that was then referred to as "Chicano," meaning community members of Mexican descent. The bank's opening was remarkable and included a Catholic Mass and a ribbon cutting by state governor John Arthur Love.

It was only a short time after its opening that Coronado began to feel pain. The unexpected death of Paco Sanchez six months into operations left the bank without its biggest champion and advocate. Sanchez's death would be just one of many problems that plagued the institution and ultimately leveled it. By June 1976, the bank was put into what is known as receivership. Under receivership, a troubled bank enters a period of protection, similar to when a business files for Chapter 11 bankruptcy protection. Coronado was then declared insolvent, and the comptroller reported that Coronado had endured operating and loan losses since the day it had opened.

All told, Coronado had about four thousand accounts, which were valued at $2.4 million. Documents revealed that 73 percent of the savings and 66 percent of the checking accounts had under $300 in them. Coronado was then liquidated, a laborious task that can take anywhere from two to five years to complete.

To liquidate, individuals file their claims with the FDIC to attain what are called receiver's certificates. The FDIC also collects information about loans due and loan payments according to the bank's original contracts and documents. Liquidation also involves the sale of any furniture or other assets within the bank, to establish a special account for its creditors. Monies raised from this account are invested in government securities that grow interest until a dividend can be declared. The ensuing payout system has a pecking order of its own. Dividends get paid out to creditors first. Then any owed bills get covered. Finally, any remaining money after that goes to the bank's stockholders.

Like Skyline, Coronado had opened with the best intentions and a mission to serve a niche population that had traditionally been overlooked. Both banks sought to empower underserved communities in the process. But rather than serve as beacons of financial empowerment, both banks had instead ended up serving as cautionary tales for anyone looking to follow in their footsteps. This included the Women's Association.

A group, no matter how earnest in approach, could not just set up a bank and hope for the best. It was the operations and policies that mattered, alongside having enough clients to keep things going. Ultimately, what plagued Coronado was a money problem. "By and large, these people never had used banking like middle class Americans do," explained Bernard Valdez, who was one of the bank's original incorporators, to the *Denver Post*. "People used the bank as a place for safe storage of their money rather than an investment opportunity."

Max Brooks, chairman of the board of Central Bank of Denver, also noted that the marketing of Coronado as a bank for a specific population segment hadn't done the bank any favors. Speaking with reporters at the *Rocky Mountain News*, he said, "If a bank gets a tag of being for one particular group, it makes it tough."

These two lessons remained top of mind as the Women's Association continued to work to set up their own bank. The failures at Coronado and Skyline also underscored a lasting sticking point that everyone was familiar with. While customers were insured, shareholder investments at failed banks were a risk that could not be guaranteed. No matter how well intentioned, something you personally believed in might still end up being an unwise investment.

CHAPTER 21

The Equitable Building

Denver's Equitable Building is a stunning, imposing nine-story structure at the corner of Seventeenth and Stout Streets in the heart of the famed Seventeenth Street financial district. On a clear day looking westward on cross streets like Stout, pedestrians and drivers enjoy a crystal-clear view of the Rockies dead ahead. The mountains have a personality of their own, sometimes appearing purplish or gray and sometimes hidden away entirely if the sky is cloudy. The modern-day Denver skyline outdoes Equitable in height, but when it was completed in 1892, it was marketed as the tallest, finest building in town, and for good reason.

On the kind of Colorado day where the sun hits it just right, the Equitable Building appears to come to life, teasing its passersby with tales of the opulence of bygone eras. On the days when it was *the* building in town, that meant business. But the Equitable Building hides its finest crown of gems from outside onlookers. These can only be enjoyed by slowing down, stepping into the building's lobby, and simply looking around or looking up. That is when everything shimmery about the building appears almost magically before the eye.

When construction began on the building in 1890, Denver had evolved just enough to see the nation's perception of it changing some too. It might have earned the local nickname of Cow Town, but in the years before and after its founding, the Greater Denver area possessed both geographical and financial appeal.

The Equitable name comes from the project's initial commissioner, the Equitable Life Assurance Society of the United States. The firm, an insurance and finance company, was founded in New York City by businessman Henry Baldwin Hyde. The New York City headquarters opened in 1870 in the New York Equitable Building, located in the financial district.

Equitable made its westward migration two decades later, when a company made up of Denver and eastern capitalists formed the Denver Equitable Building Company. The company needed a building, and they would spare no expense. Famed builders and architects Andrews, Jacques and Rantoul of Boston designed the building in the Italian Renaissance style and fashioned it with breathtaking stone and shiny marble cuttings throughout.

Its structure uses a "double E" architectural style, with natural light filtering through an endless sea of colorful, elegant Tiffany glass windows. The lobby walls and pillars are wrapped in marble of swirling yellow, gold, cream, and light-brown tones. The high, vaulted ceilings are made of white tile mosaic art and edged with shimmery gold tiles. The dark-brown marble floor alternates with panels of solid red-brown and swirling red-brown and white marble. A grand bronze staircase sits near the middle of the building, completing the lobby's opulent look.

But as anyone knows, opulence and grandeur don't come cheap. Equitable was no exception. It wasn't too long into its maiden voyage on Seventeenth Street when Equitable fell into financial trouble. It was listed for public auction on December 31, 1895. A sullen *Denver Post* speculator mused, "It is not at all probable that there will be any redemption and the property will undoubtedly fall into the hands of the New York company."

Equitable's first-floor corner unit is a functioning bank space that has seen many tenants through the years. When vacant, the space goes by unit 1C. Like Equitable itself, the walls of unit 1C also have their tales to tell. Given Equitable's height, falls—both accidental and speculative—weren't unheard of.

The case of J. S. Cathon of Cleveland, Ohio, is one such mysterious tumble. Prior to his incident, Cathon had reportedly asked the building's elevator operator about the views as they made their way up to the ninth-floor rooftop overlook. A bit of a mystery, Cathon was said to be of "ill health," and he had gone up because he wanted to see a panoramic view of the city. Later, onlookers reported spotting him sitting on the overlook's edge with his feet "hanging over the other side."

Cathon's fall was not a suspected homicide nor was it immediately ruled as an accident or a suicide. His death simply deepened the mystery of his life and the source of his fall. His body fell nearly 125 feet before landing on the skylight of modern-day unit 1C. At that time, it was home to Equitable's first banking tenant, First National Bank.

First National was an already established Denver entity when it announced plans to relocate to Equitable by January 1, 1896. The proposed new bank space would be in the building's corner unit, which was then occupied by the Philadelphia Smelting Company. Both parties agreed that Philadelphia Smelting would move from the unit and First National would remodel the space. To overhaul the unit, First National spent a reported $77,000 to transform the first floor into an elegant bank lobby and office. First National also leased a portion of the basement and made it over into safe storage that included chilled steel vaults weighing twelve tons. Its proposed January 1 opening stalled after the sourced Italian marble intended to be used in the bank's flooring proved difficult to procure, but the project continued.

At midnight on February 19, the *Denver Post* reported that two heavy draft-horse teams moved more than $5 million in client funds from the former site of First National Bank to its new home in the Equitable Building. This ceremonious analog transfer of funds was a heavily armed undertaking, "guarded by twelve Pinkertons and a score of able-bodied laborers walking behind," according to the *Denver Post*.

With its assets safely in place, the bank opened on February 24, a start that branded the bank's clerks and officers the busiest men in the city.

By the time the Women's Association considered the available bank space at the Equitable Building in 1976, the building had been sold several times. Many more long-forgotten entities and characters had passed through the doors of unit 1C. Rumors of ghosts from more fallen victims, like Andrew the window washer, who'd plunged to his death outside the building, continued to give the otherwise elegant structure an unexpected ghostly edge.

For all its victories and tragedies, secrets and opulence, the Equitable Building eventually won over the Women's Association as the perfect place to locate their bank. The charter application mandated that they list the address where the proposed bank would be. There had been weeks of back-and-forth about where they wanted to locate their bank. As far back as November 1975, whether to locate in the heart of downtown or to press to the outskirts was a much (and often) debated topic. Downtown won out and so, too, would Equitable.

Joy Burns, another established Denver mover and shaker, and a handful of others made up the group's building committee, and they toured many potential locations, reporting back their findings and recommendations to the Women's Association. The selection process had come a long way rather quickly. It wasn't that long ago when, during the meeting on February 14, 1976, no fewer than eighteen potential locations were presented with attendant commentary in the form of pros and cons. By the end of that meeting, the committee members' hard work had paid off, and the group narrowed their prospects down from eighteen to two. A negotiation committee, including Barbara Sudler and Carol Green, was formed and set out to negotiate rental terms and sign a lease. Leasing the potential site was not a straightforward task, since they didn't know when the charter would be approved or when they'd be able to open. And they certainly couldn't pay its rent in the meantime.

By the next meeting, the Equitable Building was unanimously selected as the group's first choice for a location. Once they received approval for their charter from Washington, DC, they could begin renovations on the space. Garrett-Bromfield, the firm that owned the building, would charge an average of six dollars per square foot for the space and had agreed to a one-year hold until the charter was granted. A one-year hold was important since it meant they would have the space even if charter approval hadn't yet been received. Little did they know they would have to get an extension of that hold.

It seemed like fate: the Women's Bank would make its home in the Equitable Building. It was the perfect message about the group's mission to make access to credit more, well, *equitable*.

CHAPTER 22

Those Girls

Summer 1977

They were buzzing with excitement as they gathered together in their finest outfits. Standing in the grand marble stairwell of the Equitable Building, their now-approved location to open up shop, they were so ready to pose for this publicity picture. *Finally*, their request for a national bank charter had been given preliminary approval.

Everywhere you looked that year, you could spot one of Those Girls in an instant. Some peeked out from this very group.

They smiled at you with confidence atop billboards and from glossy magazines, selling clothing, accessories, and cosmetics sure to highlight a cheekbone or bring out the shade of an eye. Having "come a long way, baby," some now faced the camera, Virginia Slims cigarette in hand, daring someone, anyone, to just try and stop them now. They fit seamlessly into the latest fashions, which sometimes included tight-fitting, bright, bold patterns and colors. No longer willing to be bound by those skirts-only dress codes that underscored their girlhoods, they might wear jeans or pantsuits while out and about as part of the mass effort to normalize two-legged ensembles once and for all. They made fashion choices whether or not the men in their lives, at home, at work, or on the street approved.

Those Girls. They poured onto college campuses in record numbers. There they demanded (and now sometimes won) women's studies courses and curriculum. These new classes helped offset the more traditional majors they once had been encouraged to pursue, like the home economics degree that Wendy Davis had received before going on to pursue her law degree. If they had children to look after, they now patchworked a childcare situation together to bridge those gaps during their time away from home. While out, they took night classes, played bridge, or maybe pursued an artistic hobby like pottery making.

Those Girls.

They ranged in age and had initially drawn some of their inspiration from the suffragettes who, half a century before, had marched in the streets and had fought for and won the vote. But now they were fighting for something else. Those Girls were updating their demands and refashioning the equality mission to better fit the modern age in which they now lived—the 1970s. They were going to fight harder to become more fully realized individuals with rights that went far beyond their grandmothers' goals. This time, they wanted lasting seats at the proverbial tables where decisions were made. As Shirley Chisholm famously said, "If they don't give you a seat at the table, bring a folding chair."

As they expected, at times their boldness was met with resistance and had to be tempered. There was still a template of sorts that most understood they had to follow if they wanted to muddle through. Anyone existing on the outskirts of that muddling through knew they would face more risk and higher stakes. The boldest of Those Girls also faced societal backlash. Advertisers on New York City's Madison Avenue might have presented a sleek, sexy archetype of the modern, independent woman, but within communities and around dinner tables, there was an unspoken understanding. Every step they took, whether they wore a leather heel, a sneaker, or an earth-toned boot, still often occurred under the umbrella of being second-class citizens in their own country. Sticking one's head above the parapet still carried a risk, because it was still ultimately a man's world.

One only needed to look at the songs on the radio for clues about how certain men felt about Those Girls. For every song by rock-and-roll sisters Ann and Nancy Wilson of Heart that embraced their position as some of Those Girls, trying to explain to their worried mothers that they couldn't escape the "magic man" with "magic hands," there was ELO growling back that she was an "evil woman" or Cliff Richard warning other men about a "devil woman" who would "get you from behind."

The group in the stairwell that day was an eclectic one. They hailed from many ideals, religions, lifestyles, and schools of thought. For months, they had fused together, calling themselves the Women's Association. Their group also included several men who believed in the venture. That venture was right in line with the progress that the new group of Those Girls had been working toward.

Inside the stairwell, excited voices echoed off the regal, swirling marble walls. They all had to admit it. After so much time, that day was a pretty wonderful day. They had begun meeting to discuss this project nearly two years prior and had hoped they'd be opening by now, but it wasn't in the cards, so they kept going. Along the way, they conquered numerous obstacles, both foreseen and unforeseen, to arrive at this moment. In those early days, they were just a band of hopefuls. They couldn't have imagined that struggles or philosophical differences might splinter them or that bureaucratic red tape might slow them down. They simply wanted to explore the idea of opening a bank that assisted *all* people, with an extra emphasis on women's specific financial needs.

It was time to take the picture.

Five women in the group sat together in a window, making up the back row, among them Carol Green, Edna Mosley, and Gail Schoettler. Gail was one of the youngest members. With her deep smile, dark pixie cut, white short-sleeved shirt, and patterned skirt, she had a long road ahead of her upon the news of bank-charter approval. Her team would head up sales of bank stock and solicit the ambitious goal of a million dollars in deposits for the bank's opening day. Her smile also hid that at home things were becoming a bit strained. Her husband's response to her participation was tepid. Tradition dictated that Saturday mornings were supposed to belong to mothers. Mothers were responsible for feeding and minding the children while fathers who had worked all week might sleep in. But if Women's Association meetings took place on Saturday mornings, babysitters and fathers had to fill in any gaps.

Judi Foster sat beside Betty Freedman. Despite their difference in age, they had become fast friends, making for a sensational pair. Betty was a Denver native who'd once dreamed of a cosmopolitan life as a writer somewhere in an East Coast city. She'd done some moving around but had ended up back home in Denver nonetheless. She was a socialite and a doctor's wife with two older children and a respected position in society. Always a sharp, eye-catching dresser, she'd muted her style some for this picture, favoring a businesswoman's look with a three-piece ensemble that included a plain skirt, dark blouse, and light-colored blazer.

Judi was a California native who had moved to Denver for her husband's job. Although married, she had chosen to work on a career. The children bit would figure itself out later. In her long-sleeved polka-dotted dress with her hands clasped in her lap, she peered up at the camera and smiled without revealing the nagging sense that something at home might be going terribly wrong. As a woman with a background in finance, Judi was the perfect fit for the bank project and had even stepped in to assist the group by leading them after things splintered. She had recently begun to work for herself, even opening her own firm. Issues at home presented a dilemma for her financial future. She would outearn her husband. If they proceeded with a divorce, he might be eligible for half of her money.

Everyone in the photo was hopeful about the direction things were headed, but perhaps the most satisfied person that day was Carol Green. This project had been her idea, hatched two years earlier during a rare idle period for her. Now her hair had begun to fade in patches, and rather than color it or cover it up, she had opted to let it continue to fade. Dressed in a short-sleeved ruffled number and her signature dark horn-rimmed glasses, her smile hid the story she always shared about her life. How when she was small, a weight problem and diet pills had wreaked havoc on both her body and her mind and how her life's triumph of losing weight and keeping it off had helped lead them to this moment.

Nearby Judi and Betty sat Wendy Davis. In her patterned shirt and blazer with her hair cut short, she was as glad as everyone else to be present in this moment. Wendy had been part of the project almost since its inception. Like Carol Green and Edna Mosley, Wendy had a front-row seat and had seen the ups and downs that came when a group looked to create something without much of a template to follow. She'd borne firsthand witness to the consequences that came after too many cooks stood in the bank project's proverbial kitchen. Wendy remained determined to see the project through because it was something she believed in. As an attorney and a member of city council, she might have been one of the closest members in that picture to resemble one of Those Girls.

In this moment, however, their personal lives didn't matter as much as their collective, building excitement. What had begun as a conversation in an elegant, spacious living room as part of a coffee-klatch subject or even an early Weight Watchers meeting was now a nationally chartered bank that would soon open its doors. The wire from Washington, DC, had come, revealing that along with a bank local to DC, the Women's Association's project in Denver had been granted permission to organize under a national charter. They were to be the first two banks of their kind given status as nationally chartered banks.

More than fifty years after that early predecessor bank run by Mrs. F. J. Runyon had opened, the 1970s had seen many new strides toward leveling the playing field for women. Even the ERA had been revived. In summer 1975, women across the globe had descended on Mexico City as part of the first International Women's Year conference, where access to adequate funds and financing were on the docket for discussion. Meanwhile, after the women's bank in Tennessee merged in 1926, there was a five-decade-long lull. Now several banks had opened to cater to women clientele. New York started the trend in 1975, quickly followed by interest in opening up similar banks in places like Connecticut back east and West Coast locales like San Diego. Now, with the announcement of the twin approvals, both Washington, DC, and Denver would be the first to be nationally chartered.

Charter approval was the main thing they had been waiting for all this time, and with it came the validation that all those meetings they'd attended and the sacrifices they'd made hadn't been in vain. With plans to open their bank later in that year or in spring 1978 at the latest, being in Equitable's stairwell meant even more to them now. Off to one side of them sat the small two-story suite they were now finally able to get in to renovate ahead of opening up. That suite represented countless hours of discussion, debate, and finally validation. With their charter approval in hand, they could actually go out into the community, sell shares of bank stock, and formally announce their arrival to the denizens of Denver.

After the obstacles they'd faced organizing the bank and with lives of their own also going on at home, nobody in that stairwell that day dared to ask what else could possibly go wrong. Nearly every woman in the photo had endured the pressure and stress that comes from being the "only one in the room," but as the only African American woman in the picture, Edna Mosley was performing double duty. She wasn't the only African American woman (or person) on the project, but she served as a reminder of the unique experiences singular to herself and to others like her in the group. The Ku Klux Klan might not have been as visible in town anymore, but racism continued to make itself known.

The Brown Palace, the famed hotel where members of the Women's Association often entertained, had once refused Edna and her husband, John, service. Just a few years prior, the city had begun to integrate its school system through a busing program. However, rather than embrace the initiative, some angry parents who didn't want that to happen chose instead to set fire to a fleet of brand-new yellow school buses in protest. Edna continued to speak out as part of the local NAACP and would continue to advise the group about how to appeal to communities that lay beyond Denver's white women and men. She posed in front of the Tiffany glass in her striking dark dress with its white collar and cuffs, her hair done perfectly. Her presence spoke of the hours she had already logged and would continue to log on the project to ensure that the African American community knew about credit and banking services too.

With the official picture snapped, charter in hand, and hope in their hearts, the group disbanded. It was time for phase two. Regardless of what was happening at home, they had their work cut out for them if they were going to open on time. Nobody on that day could have predicted that the schedule might go sideways yet again or that another waiting game might slowly erode the newly replenished hope felt on that day.

News had arrived on 7-7-77, and all sevens was a good omen.

For now, at least.

CHAPTER 23

Others Have Tried

July 5, 1977

The prior agenda for an upcoming July 9 meeting was not particularly cheerful. Thankfully, it now needed updating, but the despair is worth noting nonetheless. Judi had written, "We still have not heard from Washington, and as you know, our option on the Equitable Building space expires on August 8. We will decide upon a course of action to speed a decision at the July 9 WA meeting." The Women's Association hadn't met since May 14, because there was nothing to discuss. Many knew this process well. All they could do was wait.

And now they would be meeting to discuss another extension of their lease on space at the Equitable. In March, they had negotiated an extension on their lease option that stretched it to August 8. The rent remained six dollars per square foot. However, with the August 8 deadline looming, their hands were now tied while they waited on an update. The unit sat untouched.

By the July 9 meeting, however, the news had come through: the Women's Association had received preliminary approval. With a renewed sense of optimism and enthusiasm, they tackled the remaining items on their to-do list. The approved charter application meant the countdown to seeking permission to open and then, finally, opening day was on. After so many months of uncertainty, even the slightest inching forward was a welcome reprieve. Charter approval was a fully breathed sigh of relief. During the endless waiting, members of the Women's Association had wondered about the fate of their project. Finally, they had an answer.

The Denver group knew how lucky they were. The Washington, DC, women's bank had also applied and recently had its charter application rejected. They'd had to reapply. And the New York City bank, such a beacon at its opening, had become a cautionary tale.

Financial concerns do not always signal a death knell for a bank. The same was true for New York, but an incident that took place in August 1976 certainly contributed to its issues. Susan Salvia, a twenty-three-year-old employee, had publicly accused the bank of discriminating against her after she disclosed her pregnancy to a supervisor. Salvia, who was working to support her husband, a third-year medical student at nearby Mount Sinai Medical School, said she had shared the news of her pregnancy to be honest with her supervisor, and her honesty had cost her the job. A few months prior, Salvia had been moved from her job as a teller to that of clerk. But once she informed her supervisor that she was pregnant, the supervisor tried to move her back into the teller position. Bank tellers often spend the majority of their day standing up, but Salvia, who also suffered from varicose veins, cited discomfort with standing.

Worse still, Salvia's attorney said the supervisor had told her that she could return to work after her baby was born. However, according to her attorney, she was told for the time being, she needed to leave immediately, "since you'll be leaving in a few months anyway."

In a statement to refute Salvia and her attorney's claims, founder Eileen Preiss said the bank didn't discriminate in any way. "If a proceeding is brought, it will be adjudicated, and we feel that we will prevail," she said, as reported by the *New York Times*.

All through that summer and into the fall, dubious information began to leak out from the bank. Disgruntled employees called it a farce that was just like every other male-dominated financial institution. "Everyone who has been here from the start is altogether disillusioned," said one anonymous employee to the *New York Times*. "There's been such a massive turnover," never a good sign in business. The red flags were starting to wave in the breeze.

CHAPTER 24

Her Final Straw

LaRae Orullian was finally ready to admit it to herself: she'd had the proverbial it.

As she sank into the deep salon chair feeling frustrated and defeated, she also knew it was time to make some decisions about what to do next. The hum of the nearby round bubble hair dryers couldn't drown out her boss Herman's words during their conversation earlier.

LaRae, I'd love to, but . . .

I'd love to, but. He'd love to, but.

How many times in her career had she heard lines similar to those four horrible words, and how many times had those words ended up sealing her professional fate?

She knew what came next. He'd love to, but he simply couldn't, by which he also meant he wouldn't. And the problem was that even as he wished he could—but alas, alas—he still expected her to be okay with that. And why shouldn't he? For nearly twenty years, LaRae had made a name for herself by being just that—indispensably whip smart, reliable, and okay with it when her requests for *the* promotion were casually denied.

And what exactly had being okay with that gotten her?

It had brought her this moment of staring down yet another professional denial.

LaRae was wise to the ways of banking now. She was used to navigating the uncertain seesaw of a bittersweet career that brought her both fulfillment and the denial of her full ambition to run a bank and have the proper title and salary to match. It was a frustrating, fine dance that she had perfected over time, smoothing its roughness into a professional waltz of sorts when she had to.

Reflected in the salon mirror, there she was: those same clear, sky-blue eyes and that gentle, ready smile, with a bit of subtle makeup just to enhance her natural beauty. Makeup was often the professional woman's armor, and if she was lucky enough to be able to afford it, there might even be a wardrobe to match. In LaRae's case, that meant lots of darker calf-length skirts and matching blazers; quiet, muted blouses; the occasional patterned number or pantsuit; and, of course, sensible rounded or square-toed heels to keep her fashionable yet professional looking. But LaRae also had to account for the fact that she was tall. Not just tall tall but basketball-player tall. She couldn't completely tower over the men she worked for, so her heels remained modest in height.

She worked *for* but never quite *with* these men.

She knew they had grown to expect her not to make waves, not to argue, not to stray from the tidy confines where she was permitted to work. Recently, those confines included a tidy box of vice president, a promotion she had worked tirelessly to earn.

Being vice president at any bank, including in Denver, was still not a small feat for a woman. LaRae had been one of the first and only. Her ascent along the road to Madam Vice President had been long and twisty. It was true that, in some ways, she had been recognized by her employer. She had broken barriers and received a title and position at Guaranty that was primarily reserved for men. Many had seen her professional headshot smiling back at readers in a *Denver Post* article announcing her promotion.

Yet what was missing from the article, of course, was the long-standing agony of her professional war of attrition. The denial and the obstacles. The frustration. The thankless things she was expected to do because, despite being just as qualified—if not more so—than any man, she was still often the only woman in the room. Being the only woman also meant that in addition to her workload, she would be expected to add on those often-unremarked women-specific tasks. Things like prepare and serve the coffee or empty the men's smelly, overflowing ashtrays after their meetings ended. During those meetings, she'd do her best—not even so much as fidget—while smoke from the men's cigars enveloped the room. In the back of her mind, she knew she'd be hanging yet another work outfit on her balcony when she got home. This was part of her ritual to try and rid her clothes of some of the pungent stench of a meeting's worth of cigar smoke that they had absorbed before dropping them off at the dry cleaner.

Although articles mentioned her education, nobody outside her orbit knew how long it had taken her to achieve it. For fourteen years, she had attended night classes, taking two or three courses at a time, to get a better grip on the basics of banking first and then to specialize. When graduate school was the correct next step, LaRae applied and was accepted to Ohio State. She knew Guaranty supported its men, even sent them to get their degrees. She had shared her good news about graduate school and asked her boss if he might agree to send her too. The response had been markedly different. "We've never sent a woman," he replied curtly. This was the end of their discussion about that.

Still, LaRae trusted herself. She knew that with or without the support of her employer, graduate school was the right move for her. LaRae crafted and executed a plan B. The graduate program would have to be something that didn't interfere with her regular workload or working days. Without her employer's backing and support, she would instead study by correspondence and then use her vacation days to spend two weeks on campus at Ohio State when it was necessary for her to be there in person. LaRae would continue on this learning track for three years while also performing her full-time duties at Guaranty. Her boss acquiesced to her wish to fit in an education but made it clear that under no circumstances would Guaranty give her so much as a penny or even an extra day off to do so.

Plan B also evolved into LaRae giving a presentation to the NABW in the hope of getting a scholarship to defray some of her school costs.

LaRae's presentation had impressed the organization, and the NABW awarded her a scholarship that covered her first year of courses.

Banking and finance had long been considered boy's clubs. The few women who'd managed to gain admission into these clubs were mostly relegated to the position of "powder puff" status. The powder puffs were defined as women who did jobs that were typically done by men. Women who enter modern-day "tech bro"–laden STEM programs might find themselves among the powder puff sisterhood. Banking also fell into this category, but LaRae, like so many competent women of her day, understood that she was more than an interloping powder puff. She wasn't exactly without a voice, but at times she struggled to fully capture hers. She was also in good company among women struggling to find their places in a man's industry. Over time, she had connected with two women, Margaret Hennig and Anne Jardim, who went on to write a groundbreaking book, *The Managerial Woman.*

Hennig and Jardim became her new peers from outside the bank, and they urged her to ruthlessly evaluate her position at Guaranty. If she felt she was settling, they urged her to stop doing so. It was possible, they said, to push for more, to demand clarity about her next steps and what she could expect to come her way on the job courtesy of new titles and a few promotions.

After graduate school, LaRae used some of her personal savings to take courses so she could specialize in mortgages. Here is where LaRae Orullian began to shine and to work through what felt like a potential million-dollar idea to benefit both herself and the bank. After graduating in the top 5 percent of her class, she approached Guaranty with a carefully crafted proposal: Guaranty would open a real estate and mortgage division. She could prove it would be profitable for them, and having the right education and credentials, she knew she could run the division, if they set it up. Everyone could win with a new venture like this. She could win.

The day of her presentation, LaRae took her spot in the hazy, smoke-filled conference room. She ignored the plumes of smoke wafting toward her as the men puffed away at their cigars. With confidence and her voice as clear as a bell, she presented her case. Denver was expanding, downtown was reviving, and this undeniably profitable and valuable financial service was essentially theirs for the taking. All they needed, she explained, was a real estate and mortgage department and a competent individual to run it.

Elated by her work, she looked up. Maybe, this time, it would be different. Maybe, this time, they would see . . .

The team loved the idea. They green-lit the idea. Then and there, on the spot, she was praised for her idea, but before she could exhale, someone asked the awful question: "Who will we hire to run it?"

Had she misheard?

I will run it, she had said in her head. *Hire me, pick me, I want to do this.*

As always, they'd love to, but . . .

As always, the desired promotion and recognition didn't come. Instead of being promoted to run the department she had outlined, LaRae was given the task of helping to interview, hire, and then train the *man* who would implement her vision. It was decided. As the smoke faded and the men cleared from the room, giving her what felt like hollow congratulations and praise en route to their next appointments and martini lunches, her eyes fell to the table. The ashtrays were once again overflowing, and the men once again had left them for her to empty on her way out. As always.

Would they ever see her as an equal? A woman who not only was doing their job but, at times, was doing it better than they did?

LaRae would have to let that moment, like so many others in her career, pass if she wanted to keep her job. She had the option to complain or quit, but what good would come of that? She still had to eat. LaRae was also getting on in years, and if she wanted something better career-wise, Guaranty had made it clear in no uncertain terms that she would need a new plan. It wouldn't come through a promotion there, no matter how impressive her ideas were or how much money she helped them make.

Over time, she had become quite friendly with Dr. and Mrs. Marshall Freedman. Marshall banked at Guaranty, and like countless other patrons who'd done their banking with her, the Freedmans agreed between themselves that Miss LaRae was a swell gal. But beyond those pleasant, friendly, and professional exchanges, she had more than just a great smile and a good mind for business, as anyone who knew LaRae understood. LaRae Orullian was absolutely brilliant at banking.

Being brilliant at the job wasn't always enough for women. It didn't equal promotions for LaRae or other women like her hoping to make names for themselves in powder-puff positions. Despite efforts by the Equal Employment Opportunity Commission to thwart workplace discrimination, including in banks, information from the Government Accountability Office provided damning news about banking as a whole. The Treasury department had made "limited progress in insuring that financial institutions follow equal employment opportunity practices," wrote the agency.

An eighteen-month-long study found that the Treasury department's approach to tackling such issues was to use public relations and to rely on mostly voluntary compliance from banks, rather than to actually go in and enforce the measures. The study pointed to figures that proved employment discrimination existed against women and minorities working in the industry.

At a meeting of the Senate Committee on Banking, Housing, and Urban Affairs, Raul N. Rodriguez, a witness, testified that while the large Denver banks generally had an adequate number of women and minority employees, they held, to a large extent, positions of lower rank. Rodriguez also testified that on closer inspection of the management positions, "the pattern of discrimination is clear." He stated in an August 1976 hearing that "So long as the Treasury Department does not implement their equal opportunity responsibilities, minorities and women will continue to suffer."

The inability for women to rise in the ranks, according to Rodriguez, stemmed from a lack of effective training and because over 80 percent of the women employed in upper-management positions didn't have college degrees. Many, he said, had been promoted to their current positions from secretarial posts.

While true overall, the lack of education and experience that Rodriguez described did not apply to LaRae Orullian. She *was* qualified in terms of both her education and her experience.

In that moment in the salon chair, she couldn't remember the exact instance when Betty Freedman had first cornered her to talk about the Women's Bank, but corner her she did. Betty had strode up to her, no doubt dressed in something striking, with her hair blown out and styled and her signature smile. She had excitedly told her about this new project she was working on. A group of wonderful, diverse women from all walks of life in Denver wanted to try to open their own bank. It would be for women and run by women, Betty had explained. They wanted to prove that women could be in higher-up positions at banks and to also prove that women weren't the credit risks they were unfairly stereotyped to be. After several similar encounters with Betty, LaRae grew to expect updates from her about the bank project, perhaps even almost as much as she could expect to be passed over for that next promotion at Guaranty.

Betty had suggested that LaRae could come to a meeting sometime and see what it was all about for herself. But LaRae's loyalty to Guaranty was always at the forefront of her mind. She would politely decline Betty's invitations. She politely declined while less-educated and less-talented men wrote the bad loans that she was called in to help fix. She politely declined when the bank flew her over eight hundred miles to Waco, Texas, to try and salvage a series of bad mortgages she hadn't even written. In that instance, to the delight of management, in the process of cleaning up the mess, she had even made Guaranty some money on that bad deal. She politely declined as a first, second, and then a third new male president she had trained ended up failing at a job she knew she could do better. Politely declined, emptied ashtrays, prepared and poured the coffee she still hadn't ever tasted but was told tasted great by all who drank it. The wheel of time kept turning, clocks kept ticking, and LaRae continued to exist beneath Guaranty's glass ceiling.

But on this particular day, before sinking into the salon chair, something within reliable ole LaRae Orullian had changed. It had gotten a bit bolder. She had asked her boss Herman to go to lunch, and once she sat across from him, she made her appeal.

"I have trained every president, and some have gotten into trouble," she'd said. "Why won't you give me a chance to be the president of this bank?" She knew she could do it, or at the very least, she couldn't do any worse than the men had done.

Without hesitation, he had replied, "LaRae, you know, I would, but there are two reasons why I can't do that. For starters, Colorado's not ready for a woman bank president, and, also, you don't have any gray hair."

No gray hair?

Had she heard him right? Unlike the lack of education or professional experience cited in official studies, both of which she had in spades, what had held her back all this time at Guaranty included something so simple as the color of her hair?

Now, in the salon chair, she peered at the stylist who'd come to the seat and greeted her.

"So, what are we doing today?"

Regarding Herman's reasoning, LaRae couldn't do much to change her status as a woman, but she *could* do something about her hair. It was almost laughable. Half of her professional battle, according to Herman, could be won courtesy of a process that cost under six dollars at the drugstore, if she stood at her sink and did it herself with the help of a box of L'Oréal.

If Guaranty's customers wanted to do their more official bank business with a woman president who had gray hair and it meant she could finally be taken seriously enough to be promoted, she'd let them all have one. Locking eyes with the stylist in the mirror, she set her chin. Her dark hair refused to give up its pigment, so she'd turn to chemistry to assist and let it do the trick.

"I'd like to frost it," she said.

"Frost it all away."

CHAPTER 25

The Plans Continue

"Now all the women have to do is raise $2 million," proclaimed the August 1977 issue of *Denver Magazine* on the news that the Denver Women's Bank, NA, was officially in possession of its preliminary charter. The word was out: at long last the Women's Association had their national charter approval. Opposite a black-and-white snapshot of Judi and Paul, all smiles and sitting at a table at the long-awaited press conference, the article continued: "The prospectus for the Women's Bank, NA, is out, offering potential investors interest in the bank at $20 per share. Initial investments must be a minimum of ten shares, but increments can be purchased one share at a time after that."

With one hurdle crossed and two million things and dollars to go, this simplified description of what lay ahead wasn't exactly untrue. Now that they had the charter approval, they needed to sell their bank to the general public at twenty dollars a shot. To accomplish that feat, however, required more than simply going out and raising the money. It also involved appealing to the public through outreach and remaining transparent about the very real risk and opportunity involved. Some of the preparation took place during a three-part workshop they held that covered soliciting stock subscriptions.

"Good morning, Mrs. Jones. How are you today?"

Judi looked over at the woman across the table who would serve today as "Mrs. Jones." The woman looked down at the paper in front of her and followed the script.

"Fine," she replied.

Judi continued. "I'm calling to introduce myself. My name is Judi Foster, and I'm a member of the Women's Association, which is working to open a new bank. Do you have a minute now, or should I call you back later?"

"Now is fine," replied "Mrs. Jones," right on cue.

Thus far, things with "Mrs. Jones" were going great. Now it was time to share a few facts and to try and solicit her interest.

"Our bank is the Women's Bank, which will be located at Seventeenth and Stout in the historic Equitable Building. We will be offering services unique to this area that we feel are needed. We think many people, including you, need a financial [education] and personal attention to make pertinent decisions in the financial world. Who in your family makes financial decisions?"

Most in the room pretty much knew the answer. "Mrs. Jones" would most likely say that money in her home started and stopped with a man. Maybe with a husband or a father. If she was single, perhaps a brother or an uncle could be counted on. If she was widowed and he was old enough, her own son might be whom she had to rely on to assist with her financial matters.

There were, of course, exceptions to this expectation. In a *Denver Post* article about the newish trend of women keeping their last name after getting married, the reporter spoke with a woman named Luanne Aulepp. She had remarried later in life and reportedly had kept both her name and her financial matters separate from those of her new husband. She "wants to keep her own credit rating intact," wrote the *Post*. Regarding her financial advantage, the article continued, "as a single woman, she worked hard to convince a savings and loan company to give her a mortgage on a house. Also, she has BankAmericard and

American Express credit cards in her own name and she didn't want to lose them."

Her rare success with credit and banking accounts on her own made her an outlier among many women seeking credit. Aulepp simply summed up her sentiment on being married: "I'm married but I'm me."

For every Luanne Aulepp, there were thousands of women who had yet to feel as though their financial needs were met and their voices heard. To make the mock-call scenario unfolding in the meeting room that day more realistic, the group had come up with personality prototypes like Mandy Mother and George Gump. There was also Sally Sneed, who was described in the workshop packet as "not into Women's Lib, somewhat of a whiner," and Bo Sen, who "thinks her husband would blow his top if she even mentioned the idea, although she herself likes it"; neither was to be outdone by Sam Wilkins, who seemed "interested, but mostly in getting a date."

At the workshops, they thumbed through the prepared packets that informed them of how to reach out to potential customers and clients to tell them more about Women's Bank. Part sales pitch and part case study in human behavior, the packets detailed some ideal ways to conduct outreach. Before doing so, members would need to read over the feasibility study and to submit their biography, which was a brief account of their educational background and business and civic experience over the past five years. In addition, they were to work on submitting two sets of lists: a Blue list and a 250 list, both of which named people they knew who might be good prospects for purchasing bank stock. Anyone who fell under the Blue list was categorized as a prime prospect that the member would contact directly. Names on a 250 list were those who were prospects that the member did not necessarily want to contact directly. Upward of ten thousand names might seem like an enormous pool, but only an estimated one out of twenty contacts could be expected to actually buy stock.

"Know what motivates people," one document read, with "Maslow" underneath it and the following list, according to the hierarchy of needs:

- Gain or profit
- Power or control
- Achievement or recognition
- Self-preservation or security
- Satisfaction of senses
- Service to others

"LISTEN CAREFULLY TO THEIR NEEDS," the document added.

Perhaps wisely, the workshops also aimed to prepare the trainees to anticipate resistance. Members were advised to put themselves in the prospective client's position and ask:

- What might I not understand about my proposition?
- What might I doubt or fear?
- Why might I put off action?

Preparing for resistance was a logical, practical move, but in the end, they needn't have worried much. By the time they held workshops on August 13, a little over a month after they had received approval from Washington, DC, the group already had deposit pledges of $517,000, representing over one-fourth of their $2 million fundraising goal. Importantly, the groundwork to sell stock had been laid, and both momentum and interest continued to grow.

When the group composed their official offering circular, a document that is both filed with the comptroller and distributed to solicit funds from potential investors, they were mindful that it must be worded carefully so as not to mislead anyone.

Specific disclaimers in the literature included a notice that the investment was not insured and that nothing was guaranteed. Furthermore, payouts such as dividends were unlikely to come out of the bank in the near future, and it was not possible to determine if a market for common stock, which represented ownership or a claim on a portion of the bank, would develop.

But the circular also reminded its readers that the future of the modern workplace in downtown Denver just might be on their side. In 1975, 70,300 employees worked in Denver's Central Business District. The Central Business District would be the primary customer base for the Women's Bank, with the Greater Denver metro area serving as the secondary group—"primarily individuals, businesses, and organizations who wish to conduct business with the Bank because of its emphasis on non-discriminatory practices and the individualized services it intends to render." Even so, the circular continued:

> There can be no assurance that the bank will be successful. It generally has been the experience in the banking industry for new banks to lose money during the first year of operation and often during the second year of operation. There is no reason to anticipate that the bank will not also lose money for at least the first three years of operation . . . The Bank believes that downtown depositors will be difficult to obtain because of their reluctance to change to a new bank. The Bank further believes that its special emphasis on the needs of women and the providing of personalized, professional services will not necessarily prompt depositors in any substantial number to withdraw their accounts from competitors and deposit their funds with the Bank. Consequently the success of the Bank will depend primarily on traditional factors such as obtaining efficient, experienced, and aggressive bank management.
>
> While the bank believes that its commitment to providing such leadership will not adversely affect its level of profitability, the ability of the Bank to operate profitably

could be diminished to an indeterminable extent because of this relatively untested approach to banking.

Gail Schoettler and Carol Green joined forces to design the bank's first deposit form, one that was distributed to interested parties in the hope of getting the pledges that would help them reach their $2 million goal. Gail had also worked on the design of an official brochure. A trifold 8½" x 11" black-and-white, double-sided trove of information about the coming bank had a picture of a Victorian woman on the cover. "WOMEN BELONG IN THE HOUSE!" it said in big, bold letters above the picture. Below the picture, in smaller letters, the brochure cover added "AND THE SENATE!" And on the final line: "AND NOW IN BANKING!"

The day after the group announced charter approval, the Equitable Building received landmark designation. Shortly thereafter, the remodel for the Women's Bank in the newly vacated space had begun. This bank would represent dreams and good fortune, and rather than invest too heavily in ornate trappings, the group would rely on the lobby and their presence in Equitable itself to send out a message of opulence. The Women's Bank would create a functional, comfortable space that worked within their budget and image.

Inspired by Mrs. Roebling's influence over the layout of Trenton Trust and her penchant for making banks accessible, comfortable, and approachable, the teller walls would come down, and glass windows would be removed. In their place would be an open-floor concept with countertop spaces for clients to interact with bank staff and management more personally. They stuck to their thrifty budget when it was time to furnish the offices in the upstairs mezzanine portion of the bank, opting for functional and modest furnishings, which included bright, comfortable chairs, sturdy tables, and useful cabinetry.

The group had also managed to secure an information line with the last four digits 2265, which spelled out "BANK," adding an easy publicity tool to the venture.

And stock continued to sell.

Some of the most eyebrow-raising news about the New York City bank had come in September 1976 when rumors swirled that Madeline McWhinney was leaving her post early. She was reported to be breaking her five-year contract to take a position as a lecturer in the MBA program at New York University. Speaking to members of the press anonymously, insiders said that McWhinney had vacated her office several months prior and "confided that she was dissatisfied with the way the [bank] was being run." Sources also said that there was a sense of "isolation from doing anything at the bank" and that she was often sent on trips to represent the bank and try to win new customers.

Spokespeople denied these claims, stating McWhinney was on vacation and would return to the office the second week of September.

McWhinney did ultimately leave and was replaced by Lynn D. Salvage, a thirty-year-old with experience as a vice president at Bankers Trust Company and degrees from the University of Pennsylvania and Harvard Business School. When Salvage took over, it became clear that the bank would need to undergo intense changes if it was to survive. It had reported net losses of $938,521 for 1976, which was atop the losses of $565,813 in 1975. Salvage set to work to recoup the losses and trim costs. Staff was cut to twenty-seven members, from forty-three at the bank's peak, and the costly technology and risky loans in its portfolio came under scrutiny. Fixing these financial woes would not be easy.

For all that it had hoped to provide consumers, the once-strong First Women's Bank in New York City now appeared to be limping along. Other banks planning to open looked at it closely, to learn from its mistakes. One of the biggest challenges for any bank is whether enough of its stock will sell. Only the general public can answer that riddle. Like the group in New York, the Women's Association believed in banking on the spirit of sisterhood, with the occasional ally from the brotherhood thrown in the mix for extra good measure. Along the way, the Women's Association took notes about what had gone well and what had gone sideways in New York. But as the next women's bank to open, they also knew the whole world would be watching women's banks a bit more closely after the splashy opening and headline-inducing incidents over at their New York sister.

Everyone hoped things could straighten out for the New York bank group. This wasn't a contest between rivals. If any women's bank succeeded, it would help to prove that they, too, could do it. But the reverse was also true: if it failed, it would be that much harder for the Women's Bank in Denver to be approved.

During the final few months of preparation to open, their speaking engagements and workshops began as a prelude for potential clients of what was to come. In one instance, Mrs. Roebling presented and praised hardworking women: "Working women will be the most significant and influential factor in the American economy in the last half of this century—by the year 2000 not only will women benefit, but also the entire economy," she said at an address. "Everybody and everything stand to gain by the enormous growing dollar power of the American woman."

The delay the group had suffered through while waiting for charter approval hadn't turned out to be a complete waste of their time either. Those extra months gave them opportunities to have deeper discussions about their organization plans. They also had a chance to conduct more research into the relatively new phenomenon known as EFT. Adding EFT service would completely modernize and automate the process of transferring funds.

To conduct an EFT, a digital medium, such as a phone, serves as the middleman between a consumer and their bank. EFT enables the transfer of money from one party to another without requiring paper or even having to set foot in a bank. For instance, consider an employer offering employees direct-deposit services. EFT enables the employer to transfer funds directly to the employee's bank account. In its infancy, the EFT process had its share of skeptics. Consumer concerns included client privacy, account security, potential for malfunction, and the need for legal receipts. The EFT process looked and sounded convenient, but because it was still untested for the most part, its impact on the industry and, in turn, the economy remained a big question mark.

After much discussion, the Women's Association decided that despite any skepticism or potential risk, the EFT revolution was impossible to ignore; although new, it was still the way many banks looking toward the future were headed. They understood that subscription to an EFT system was probably a necessary move if they wanted to compete in the market. EFT could give them an edge in appealing to potential clients from outside the downtown Denver area as well. "We need to carefully consider this, especially since it could enable us to get to suburban locations," wrote the recording secretary at a meeting.

Meanwhile, more stock sold.

CHAPTER 26

Opening Day

BANK PRESIDENT

CHIEF EXECUTIVE OFFICER
Preliminary charter application approved for the
Women's Bank, NA 17th St. location. Denver.
Organizer invites C.E.O. applications from quali-
fied M/F candidates. Confidentiality assured. Please
send resume to the Women's Bank, NA (Organizing)
Brooks Tower, Suite 27C. 1020 15th St. Denver,
Colo. 80202
Equal Opportunity Employer
—From a want ad in the *Denver Post*, 1977

Denver, Colorado
Morning of Friday, July 14, 1978

When the job offer came in the fall of 1977, LaRae was abroad on a
golf trip. A letter from the group arrived to her room at London's Drury
Lane Hotel:

Please let this letter serve as an offer from the Board
of Directors of the Women's Bank, NA to employ you

in the official capacity of President, Chief Executive Officer, and a Director of the bank.

Terms included a $40,000 base salary with annual increases determined by the board of directors, a moderately priced car of her choosing and related expenses, membership to a country club, a business (dining) club downtown of her choosing, professional memberships and other related expenses, an expense account, and four weeks of paid vacation. As compelling as the offer was, LaRae also knew it presented her with a dilemma: to stay at Guaranty or to go with the Women's Bank.

With a deep breath and paper in hand, she made what accountants and bankers refer to as a "T account." A T account consists of drawing intersecting horizontal and vertical lines on a page to form a T. In one column go the pluses, or assets. In the other column go the minuses, or liabilities. This exercise, although simple, serves accounting practices well and brings clarity. Sometimes LaRae had also used it when faced with a dilemma or difficult decision about her life. This offer from Women's Bank was the perfect opportunity to utilize this professional tool in her personal life.

She sat and drew her columns. Thinking it over, she began to fill them up. As she scratched away her thoughts, a curious pattern emerged. She came out even on the bottom. Both sides were equal. So she ran it again, hoping for a different outcome, only to end up with the same results. It turned out that the practicalities of staying at Guaranty matched the adventure of going with Women's Bank.

Stalemate. Draw.

Staying with Guaranty was no guarantee of going higher professionally and leaving it came with risk, and LaRae understood that risk held a different meaning for men than it did for women. To a man, taking any risk meant there was still a chance for a possible reward. Men could and did fail upward all the time. She'd seen firsthand that the world wasn't always so kind to a woman in the same position. Taking a risk equaled putting both her career and her reputation on the line.

One night, as she sat turning over the issue in her mind, the answer came to her.

Here you are telling others to take opportunities when they come, and you are passing up the opportunity of a lifetime. As a child, she had scaled silvery cherry trees, shimmied out onto limbs, and picked their fruits without fear. By accepting this offer, she would be going out on another limb, perhaps with slightly more fear than back when she was traipsing through the cherry orchards of Salt Lake, but here she was with an opportunity yet again to take a risk, go out on the limb, and see about plucking that reward.

And besides, she had already proved that she couldn't do any worse for the bank than what a man might do.

On this pleasant midsummer morning, a million dollars in deposits was the goal for the day. It had all been a bit of a blur since LaRae had agreed last fall to sign on as president and CEO of the Women's Bank. She had been the missing, final piece of the puzzle and had slotted herself in well and easily by heading up meetings and offering her advice and expertise.

LaRae had once made a statement when she left Salt Lake, and by joining the Women's Bank, she was doing so again. This time it was to her former employer and unlike any she had made before. Leaving Guaranty meant leaving a twenty-year career. Her new, frosted hairstyle was just a little bonus she'd picked up on the job there. She had chosen to keep her hair frosted as part of her statement, and now she was proof that Denver could indeed handle a woman running a bank, even if her gray hair was a dye job.

In the rush of press attention that followed her acceptance of the job, more of her life became common knowledge. Reporters seemed to relish the story of a Mormon-raised former messenger girl from Salt Lake who'd opted to travel east and seek her fortune through a career. That she had worked her way through school and slowly but surely to the office of president and CEO put her in even higher esteem. Even though her former employer would probably never admit it, B. LaRae Orullian was undeniably their most successful female alumna.

She would never forget the moment she announced her acceptance of the offer from the Women's Bank. She had walked in, frosted hair and all, and explained her stance about wanting more from her job at Guaranty. Then, before the routine hemming and hawing could begin, she shared the news about the job she had just accepted at the now-forming Women's Bank. They had offered her a position that included titles like CEO and president, and it came with perks. LaRae watched as the men who had once denied her rightful promotions suddenly changed their tunes faster than a child leapt up to change the channel on the family room TV dial when their favorite program was on. Previously, they'd *wanted* to give her the promotion but . . . And now they cast themselves in the roles of the injured parties. If she left, they'd said, she'd be hurting them on a deep, personal level. She would also be hurting the bank!

And hadn't the bank been like a family to her for all these years?

Beneath the wailing about family, it wasn't just LaRae's departure that Guaranty would have to worry about. In the two decades she had spent walking the floors front-row center at Guaranty, she had built up a roster of loyal, devoted customers. They came into Guaranty expecting to do their banking with Miss LaRae. If she left, the top brass at Guaranty had to wonder if these clients who felt loyalty to her might walk right out the door with her. Both the NABW and the Denver Downtown Business and Professional Women's Club celebrated her promotion and supported her decision to move.

LaRae's choice to go to Women's Bank also sent shock waves through the Denver banking community. Her reach extended outward to other skilled women working at Denver banks, some of whom shared her frustration about how their own careers were going. In LaRae, they had a tangible example they could follow straight out the front doors and up Seventeenth Street to potentially greener pastures. Pastures that promised to be more women-centric and friendlier toward their chances of promotion. With tension mounting at the news of her departure, some managers did damage control by calling their female employees into their offices to have a little chat.

Some women were told they had better not, under any circumstances whatsoever, get any ideas and follow her lead. Other women were asked point-blank what they needed to stay happy and stay put. It seemed that with her lone, publicized acceptance, Denver's banking rumor mill kicked into high gear. LaRae, usually quiet and out of the limelight, became a celebrity of sorts, and she was somehow bringing the hallowed, moneyed establishment of Seventeenth Street to the brink of (gasp) having to change on their own or risk losing their overlooked women employees. If they owed their women employees better and knew it, some banks made good on their professional debts right then and there.

Skeptics also had their say. Some banks claimed that women didn't need their own banks and that women clients were satisfied with their current offerings and services. Rumors swirled that naysaying men who refused to support the Women's Bank threw up their hands, muttering "let the little girls play with their dolls then."

But the members of the Women's Association weren't little girls, and Women's Bank was not their doll. People were taking it seriously and not just within the bank group's inner circles. By April 1978, their initial stock offering had completely sold out, without an underwriter and just six months after they had officially opened it to the public for purchase. Other women's banks, like the bank in New York, had struggled to sell their stock and, in turn, had spluttered after opening. This struggle was a bittersweet one to consider because it proved Carol Green's point during the rift all those months ago when they had looked to the New York City bank's opening. It also showed that the appetite for Women's Bank stock was stronger in Denver, where consumers were ravenous for the opportunity, snapping up Women's Bank stocks at ten dollars a share.

LaRae had also learned a few things in all her years in Denver. All the accolades, degrees, appointments, and certifications had finally come to fruition with her new position.

"We're not out to topple the giants of Seventeenth Street," she had said in a press conference at the Denver Country Club, one of her first after joining Women's Bank. "We believe we can add another dimension of banking."

That new dimension was something undeniably handed down from the women in banking who'd gone before them, like Mrs. Mary Roebling and Mrs. F. J. Runyon before her. Perhaps some of it had been forgotten when the boy's club took over after the war, but now it was getting dusted off and refreshed. It was to be part of the Women's Bank's message and image. They were to be what the *Denver Post* described as the "new girl network." And beyond the expected services, professionalism, and respect for individuals, they wanted to be a friend to their clients and to "provide a warm, comfortable, convenient atmosphere in which all customers feel special and at ease."

LaRae immediately understood the bank's mission and how to be both professional and accessible within it. She had joined with her new colleagues to give speeches and share information about the bank and its goals and to let people know the doors would soon open. The group's emphasis on being an equal opportunity entity specializing in getting women access to the credit they deserved or helping them to establish the credit they needed seemed to resonate with the public.

As part of the Equal Credit Opportunity Act, which had taken effect in 1975, banks and other financial institutions such as department stores and oil companies had sent over three hundred million notices to women informing them that they could now rightfully apply for credit or accounts in their own names. The result had been dismal, with only 9 percent of the recipients responding, according to the Commercial Credit Corporation.

But in Denver, things were heating up, and eligible women were excited. After a luncheon where some of the Women's Bank women spoke, Joan White, editor of the *Denver Post's* Living '77, a catch-all life-style section, felt compelled to write an op-ed in response to her experience. "The voices were feminine but the topics were money, power, institutions," she wrote. "The symbolism that sent waves through the luncheon one hopes will do so throughout the community."

White noted the sacrifices women had made by taking a chance on the Women's Bank. "Careers were important enough for some of these women to sacrifice their marriages. One woman attributed her divorce to the pressures of her job. An [unnamed] attorney said her marriage was dissolved when she refused to leave her prestigious position in Denver when her husband wanted to take a job elsewhere."

The public's interest in the venture was also invaluable, especially because the group *wanted* public input. Around the time they began to remodel their suite in the Equitable, they held an open house to encourage members of the public to provide their recommendations for the bank.

And now, as the spokeswoman for the bank, LaRae could also share the news of its ambitious plan, spearheaded by Gail Schoettler, to raise $1 million in deposits on opening day.

They had waited longer than they'd hoped for this moment. Approval from Washington, DC, had finally come the day prior: "Charter issued authorizing 'The Women's Bank, NA' number sixteen thousand seven hundred twenty-three to commence business July 14, 1978. Charter will be mailed."

Upon the announcement of permission to open, reactions in the press were plentiful and somewhat mixed. In a *Rocky Mountain Journal* article the same day, Marilyn Barnewall, who worked for United Bank of Denver, expressed mixed feelings about the bank while wishing them well all the same.

"Any bank which tells a minority segment of a society 'you're not being treated fairly and we're going to treat you right' can really be fooling them," read the article. "Credit," Barnewall said, "always is discriminatory in that everyone must meet the requirements in order to qualify. Minority banks can't serve 'bad risk' groups any better than other banks can. There is a strong potential for backlash if the bank is not operated professionally so that the minority does not end up feeling betrayed by you."

In a rebuttal, Judi made the bank's intentions clear. "We certainly do not want to mislead anyone." Critics, she said, may be forgetting that institutions named Cattlemens Bank or Merchants and Marine Bank are not automatically assumed to be playing favorites for these groups. "At least they [women turned down by the Women's Bank] will get the service of finding out how to get credit," Judi commented.

They would live with the mixed reactions. They couldn't do much about that, and they had other priorities to focus on, including opening up. They hoped opening day was going to be more than a success; they were aiming for something spectacular, a blowout. Even with just the fifty founding members, it was already going to be a large party, but they had also done so much outreach as well. Part of that outreach had included jam-packed schedules of events where they formally introduced themselves to Denver as ambassadors of the Women's Bank. A few nights before, they had held one of their many opening celebration receptions, and this morning's festivities would include balloons, cake, champagne, and a choir performance to echo off the marble in Equitable's elegant lobby.

To frugally announce their arrival in local papers, the group had also done something equal parts genius and unconventional. Ahead of the opening, rather than take out costly full-page ads in the local papers and magazines, they had sent out a lot of press releases. When it was time to advertise in the paper, they turned to the community of Seventeenth Street and beyond, inviting them to take out ads to welcome Women's Bank as the new gal on the block.

As a result, major local players like Coors took out full-page ads. "The success of the Women's Bank is important to all of Colorado" declared the black-and-white ad with a simple drawing of a woman executive sitting behind a desk counseling a couple.

The bank's double-heart logo, which consisted of two hearts, one bigger and the other smaller, spelling out "WB" when tipped at a certain angle, was prominently displayed on all the ads as well, including the full-pager taken out by the restaurant owners of downtown Denver, who declared they had "no reservations about the Women's Bank."

Suite 1C has an enormous, dark brass front door that opens onto Seventeenth Street. To commemorate the bank's opening, an elegant ribbon had been laced across it, and scissors were procured to assist with the ribbon cutting. Judi and LaRae would do the ceremonious honors. At a nearby table, several bottles of champagne sat, chilled and waiting. The bank space would soon be filled with customers, and the morning's visitors would undoubtedly spill out into the Equitable's roomy lobby. But here and now, this was one of their last moments of calm before the crowd came in.

And in that calm, everything about these women and their work together reflected back on them. It shined as only the satisfaction of reaching a light at the end of a long tunnel can.

Despite being from different walks of life, from housewife to college professor, they had still walked this path together. They had united behind a common goal, working through every disagreement, every frustration, every closed door or locked window, and had transformed a vague idea into a real, functioning bank. They had been teammates, each bringing her (or his) knowledge and strengths to the endeavor. But more than that, they really liked one another. They had become more than colleagues. They had also become friends. These friendships would last throughout the life of Women's Bank and in its aftermath. Some who remained in Denver would continue to meet up regularly as the years passed.

A line had begun to form outside the bank, and it was nearly time to cut the ribbon, open up, and start the day. It already looked promising. Yes, there were women in line, but there were also plenty of men on hand, including what looked like some father-daughter duos. One woman in the line had gotten up early to drive two hours into Denver to be part of the opening-day festivities, her daughter would remember.

During a recent talk about the bank, Mrs. Roebling had pointed to the financial injustices women still faced, starting with them only earning fifty-nine cents on the dollar when compared to what a man earned. Roebling considered this a weakness in the economy and stressed that strengthening it would benefit everyone. "Women will benefit but the greater beneficiary will be our total economy, the whole nation," she said during a Rotary Club luncheon where Joan White was in attendance to report on the event for the *Denver Post's* Women's View column. "The real payoff will come when the business community itself takes action to rectify the situation and to help give the nation the full benefit of women's dollar power."

Denver had also grown on Mrs. Roebling. In a *Denver Post* write-up about her arrivals and departures, she praised the community for its farming, mining, and construction starts, declaring the area the "right place for a new bank." She expected the men of Denver to take full advantage of Women's Bank without qualms about doing business with women. "After all, they confide in their mothers; in tight spots, they turn to the advice of their wives, and they are always defending their sisters," she'd said.

As Judi and LaRae posed for the newspaper cameras near the not-yet-cut ribbon, the pride and excitement between them swelled. A welcome reception scheduled for that evening had already received fifteen hundred RSVPs, and the one for the following day had one thousand confirmed RSVPs. Later, when they tallied the final deposit receipts for opening day, they would finally know if their million-dollar deposit goal had been lofty or practical. They had a great deal of faith in their community, but still, a million dollars was a lot of money. In 1978, $1 million was roughly equal to $4.6 million today.

After exchanging a few words of encouragement, they were ready to open the doors. There was no turning back after this. They would either crack into those seven figures or go "play with their dolls" as some of the men had sneered. But even if the start was slow and the till's count at the end of the day came up short of their goal, it might be a disappointment but it wouldn't discourage them. It would propel them to keep trying, to stay on the message of being a friend and of service to the financial needs of the community.

And for one former Salt Lake City messenger girl turned CEO and president, it was the morning of her career lifetime. LaRae hadn't made the coffee today nor had she been expected to empty a smelly, cigar-filled ashtray. She hadn't done either thing in months. She would go on to tell other women not to make coffee for anyone if they didn't want to. They weren't a boy's club bank; they were the Women's Bank of Denver in the historic Equitable Building, and now it was time to get on with it. They had work to do.

Someone had taken a peek outside and reported back immediately that a line—a longish line, even—was forming outside that morning. Would Denver come through for her and for her colleagues?

It was time to find out.

As she had done all those years ago on the train platform in Salt Lake when she suddenly knew she must break off her engagement, LaRae had come to another groundbreaking, pivotal life moment. She took a deep breath, and in a nod to her faith, she said a quick prayer. Then she nodded toward Judi confidently, her sky-blue eyes sparkling in sweet anticipation. Anything, anything at all could happen now.

It was finally time to open the front door.

It was finally time to meet the awaiting Denver crowd.

EPILOGUE

By the time the Women's Bank founders closed and locked the front doors late in the afternoon on July 14, 1978, the final till surpassed the group's initial goal of $1 million in deposits. With dust whipping its way along Seventeenth Street, the group inside the corner suite could finally exhale. One article speculated that drawing such a crowd must have been because the bank was giving away their money, but the Women's Association and everyone who had participated that day knew differently. Opening day had been a success.

In the months and years that followed, B. LaRae Orullian continued to lead the bank, which saw tremendous success. By December 1981, it had over five thousand accounts and resources totaling over $25 million. In the eighteen months following opening, Women's Bank formed a holding company called Equitable Bankshares of Colorado and opened a drive-through "motor bank" to serve its clients. LaRae's meticulous attention to detail and penchant for numbers made it possible for Women's Bank to avoid many financial pitfalls, including writing bad loans. As it grew, Women's Bank went on to fund projects that still stand today, including Tattered Cover Book Store and Wynkoop Brewing, a brew pub owned by Colorado governor John Hickenlooper. LaRae's sober approach to lending money helped to grow the bank into a thriving contender on Seventeenth Street. Rather than "play with their dolls" as some men had once suggested, Women's Bank avoided financial red flags and even went on to buy up some of the male-run banks that fell onto hard times while Women's Bank thrived. When the lease at the Equitable Building ran out, they moved locations across the street to the Ideal Building, an elegant, historic bank structure complete with marble teller windows and high ceilings, and that truly put them on the map as a resounding success.

LaRae kept her hair frosted, and her career continued to take off. Although she did not marry or have a family, she became a de facto den mother to thousands of young girls through her support and involvement with the Girl Scouts of the USA (GSUSA). At a time when the nation was still figuring out where it sat with matters of diversity, equity, and inclusion, LaRae proclaimed that GSUSA should be for all girls, regardless of race, religion, or creed. Her success and leadership brought her onto many stages, platforms, and podiums, where she continued to speak about women, careers, and money. A few decades after her "stop-over" in Denver on the way to New York City, LaRae also finally got to Wall Street. There she learned, perhaps disappointingly, that the opening bell at the stock exchange was actually a button that one pressed.

Part of the fruits of her success involved custom building her own home, located on a golf course and surrounded by luscious plants in nearby Lakewood. The occasional thwack from a stray golf ball on the course echoes off her roof eaves, and ever the entrepreneur, she jokes about taking the golf balls and selling them back to golfers by the bucketful. Although now retired from the regular workforce, LaRae continues to work toward more equity for women and marginalized groups and splits her time between Colorado and Palm Springs, California.

Mary Eckels was instructed to find a backer and then to apply for a loan at Women's Bank. She found a backer and secured the necessary loan that transferred Gusterman Silversmiths to her. In the 1980s, she was commissioned to create Women's Bank logo merchandise that included hat-pins and pendants for employees to thank them for their loyalty. Eventually, she paid the loan back to Women's Bank ahead of time. Her shop remained at the Larimer Square location until 2022, when she moved. Mary now works in a by-appointment-only workshop and out of her home.

Carol Green continued to speak in front of audiences and on stages throughout her professional tenure and even after retiring. Her story touched many lives and inspired countless women to rethink their relationships to their bodies, to food, and to themselves. She eventually sold her Weight Watchers franchise, and she and Jules left Colorado and retired to Sarasota, Florida. Carol and Jules enjoy traveling, and because she continues to stay busy and is involved in the local arts scene, they enjoy taking in shows and events. Carol continues to stay abreast of entrepreneurial adventures and enterprises that pique her interest. She remains resolute in feeling proud of her involvement with Women's Bank and still encourages women of all ages to know what they want to say or to find out and then to pipe up often. Ever the health enthusiast, Carol wakes up early, and her morning routine isn't complete without quality time spent on the treadmill. Carol continues to proudly sport her white head of hair and svelte arms.

Judi Foster (now Wagner) continued her work as a successful financial entrepreneur and as a registered investment advisor. Never one to slow down, she eventually became more involved in politics and active in her community. Throughout the '80s, she joined forces with several movers and shakers (some from Women's Bank) and formed a group called "The Velvet Hammer." Together, they went to prominent businesses around Denver to apply friendly pressure and encourage the business owners to consider putting eligible and qualified women on their boards. If they were given the excuse that no eligible women could be found, they presented the leadership with a list of eligible, qualified women who could do the job. A few years into her time with Women's Bank, Judi, by then divorced, sat beside a handsome man at an information session. It turned out that they shared a liking for the same drinks and struck up a conversation. That handsome man became her second husband, and they had a daughter, born in 1986. Now retired and widowed, Judi lives in the Denver area, where her home overlooks stunning mountain views and she tends to a rescue dog, Simba, introduced to her by her daughter.

Edna Mosley continued to work as a vocal force for Denver's minority community. Among her many accolades through the years, she became president and chairman of the board for Sister Cities International, leading a delegation on trips to Nairobi, Kenya, and accompanying the governor on a trade mission to China. Edna served twelve years on the Aurora City Council and was a fierce supporter of organizations like the NAACP. Her teammate and husband, John, continued to champion and advocate for African Americans to enter the aviation field. The flight school they founded, Mile High Flight, continues to run headed by their son, Eric Mosley, who is also a pilot. Their daughter, Edna, is a retired flight attendant who lives in the Denver area. Edna died in 2014, and John followed her a year later. In 2015, Aurora opened a new public school near East Second Avenue and Airport Boulevard named the Edna and John W. Mosley P-8 School in their honor.

Dr. Gail Schoettler always turned to her ability to help rally with others to create social change. In the 1980s, she took those skills with her and entered the political arena. She served Colorado as state treasurer starting in 1986 and was elected lieutenant governor of Colorado from 1994 to 1998. Gail continues to support electing and appointing more women to places and spaces of leadership, including public office through Electing Women, an organization she founded. Gail is an avid traveler with a robust passport and recently began taking travelers on trips to far-flung locations. Each year, she also makes her annual pilgrimage to the family ranch in Shandon, California, which members of the Sinton family continue to own and work to this day.

Betty Sue Freedman remained active on Denver's social scene. Of all the accomplishments in her life, she considered her involvement with Women's Bank as one of her finest. She went on to host a delegation during the nation's "ping-pong diplomacy" era, which brought Chinese table tennis players to Denver in an exchange program that aimed to foster better relations between China and the US. Betty was the first Jewish member to serve on the local debutante ball board and urged the organization to open its doors to minorities to create a more diverse group. She became dear friends with Mary Roebling. Knowing Mrs. Roebling also meant having someone to visit when she went to one of her favorite places on earth, New York City.

Mary Roebling remained a national face and beloved mentor to the women behind Women's Bank. During her time with them, she purchased a condo in Brooks Tower, then the tallest building in the Denver skyline, and made the Mile High City one of her homes. Always a believer in women and their ability to lead and collaborate to make lasting change for the better, she gave speeches from coast to coast throughout her life. In 1983, she put her name, Roebling, on display and proudly served as a grand marshal in honor of the one-hundredth anniversary of the Brooklyn Bridge. Mrs. Roebling died in 1994 at the age of eighty-nine, leaving behind a thick résumé and a legacy whereby banks could and should act as the department stores of finance and where financial acumen could appeal to women more easily. The building at 20 West State Street in Trenton, New Jersey, bears her name as the Mary G. Roebling Building.

Bonnie Andrikopoulos continued to advocate for underserved and marginalized groups. One of her first projects after leaving the Women's Association was to help start up a program that worked to give money to groups in need. Throughout the years, she continued to be a force in activism endeavors. Bonnie lives in Santa Fe, New Mexico.

Like most of her peers involved with Women's Bank, Wendy Davis remained a fierce advocate for the underserved, including women. She put her no-nonsense, practical lawyer's mentality to good use in many ways, including helping women in the middle of divorce proceedings, to make sure they received what they were legally entitled to. She also served as president of the Colorado Women's Bar Association, where she helped set up a partnership with Women's Bank that brought Supreme Court justice Sandra Day O'Connor to town.

In 1994, under the administration of President Bill Clinton, Women's Bank, which was still a success, underwent a transformation. That year, Women's Bank and its holding company, Equitable Bankshares, was sold to Colorado Business Bank for $17.5 million. Its acquirer and the story therein created a great deal of buzz because the new owner decided it was time to remove the word "Women's" from the title. In 1997, LaRae Orullian came full circle when she departed the bank to serve in the role of vice chairman of the board of directors at Guaranty. Although the name and ownership have changed since that hot July day in 1978, the bank continues to exist, and some original Women's Bank clients continue to have their money and accounts there.

Throughout my time on this project, I've met with many fellow women who, despite publicized steps financial institutions have taken to democratize finance, continue to feel left out of the conversation entirely. I am grateful to them for their honesty and experiences, which bolster my beliefs that this remains is our struggle and we can't stop sharing these stories, taking inspiration from women like the group in Denver, and pushing for a more level financial playing field.

ACKNOWLEDGMENTS

My personal involvement in telling the story about Women's Bank reaches back to 2016, when my friend Karen Cahn put me in touch with Saira Rao and Carey Albertine, who were looking for someone to research and write this story.

Saira and Carey chose me to tell the story and put me in touch with my amazing agent, Jess Regel of Helm Literary. Jess not only held my hand through many revisions and attempts to craft a book proposal, she assured me this was going to happen, and as luck would have it, she was right.

Saira and Carey also put me in touch with the women who became key players in the story. In spring 2017, I first met with LaRae Orullian, Gail Schoettler, and Judi Wagner for preliminary interviews. Those initial conversations inspired the proposal, and I am grateful to them for their candidness and their trust.

LaRae was open and honest about her life and her experiences, and I enjoyed spending an afternoon together at her home, looking over her memorabilia and talking about her life in more depth. There is so much more to her than I could have ever put into a book such as this, and I hope what is here does her a little bit of justice.

Gail Schoettler shared invaluable insight about not just her life, but about what it meant to be a student and a young woman in the 1960s when things were beginning to stir on the social-change front. Gail also gave me Carol Green's name as a prospective interviewee, which is how I met the woman who started it all up in her living room.

Judi Wagner proved to be an essential resource for my research efforts throughout the entire process. During the thick of COVID-19 lockdowns, she copied and sent me stacks of minutes and other useful foundational documents. When we were in person, she remained kind and a resource, putting me in touch with several other members and their children.

Carol Green helped me better understand the foundational moments in the project and inspired me to dig deeper and find my own inner confidence and to speak up more clearly.

Wendy Davis provided me with necessary background and guidance about her life and the heist in 1974. We enjoyed some laughs together during our time spent sharing this part of the project, and her encouragement stuck with me throughout.

Edna Futrell (daughter of Edna Mosley) was introduced to me by Eric Mosley. She was an absolute dream throughout my journey, even from afar when the world shut down. Her willingness to share her family's collection of artifacts and mementos from the Women's Bank along with her parents' stories were equal parts information and inspiration. I also owe you nail clippers; please come collect on that anytime.

The stories and feedback I received from Jon and Tracy Freedman (Betty's children) also helped me re-create the woman she was, and whom they no doubt miss now and forever.

Thora Aarvig, Bonnie Andrikopoulos, Lynda Johnston, and Beverly Martinez-Grall each took time out of their lives to connect with me. I am grateful to them for their help and their time; Mary Eckels also spent time telling me her story and showing me how she drew and then poured the notable double heart logo into sterling silver molds. Thank you for my necklace. I will treasure it always.

The Women's Bank archive, located at the Denver Public Library, is tended to and well kept by a team of lovely, professional folks who helped me out, stayed cheerful and friendly, and even remembered my face after enough visits out there. I would also like to thank the circulation desk at the Bud Werner Memorial Library for giving me a library card and with that, access to *Denver Post* archives that reach back into the 1800s.

Sam Freedman of the Columbia Book Seminar let me audit his class, which helped me in ways I am still grasping on to. Our offshoot group of seminar graduates, the Freedmanites, also helped me get there. Thank you, Alice, Chris, Dina, Elizabeth, Joan, Jonathan, and especially to Karen Pinchin for the support and sprints together and Lizzie Stark for showing me how to slice and dice my work on your guest room walls. We are doing it, y'all!

My team at Little A, Laura Van der Veer, who saw the potential in this proposal and took it to the next level, along with taking a journalist and chiseling out an author of sorts; Emily Murdock-Baker, who sat with me poring over many a chapter at the Marlton and on Zoom, advising on how to pull more narrative. I am also grateful to the production team, which includes copyeditors, proofreaders, fact-checkers, and their colleagues.

I extend gratitude to my own women's association as well. Theresa Walsh-Giarrusso, who looked after James while I did my research and writing; Stacey Cermack, Samantha Chipetz, and Amber Taylor, who read early pieces and gave constructive feedback; Larissa Chimelweski and Kate Glass, who always had a friendly smile for me whenever I was in Denver and we had occasion to meet up; and Chenoa Taitt and Patricia O'Connell, who told me long ago it was possible to be a mom and a writer and to make a living at it.

Saving the absolute best for very last, to my husband, Bernard, I love you and am so glad you're on this ride with me. I wouldn't want anyone else by my side during this adventure. And to James, who has spent over half his life hearing Mom go on about this book, thank you for taking care of me and going easy on me during my deadlines. Team James and Mom is my favorite.

All told, there were fifty founding members involved in opening up the Women's Bank. They are as follows: Earl M. Baldwin, Jeanne E. Balkin, Betty B. Berris, Norma E. Besant, Joy S. Burns, Suzanne Spitz Carmichael, Patricia J. Clark, Leslie Davis, Wendy W. Davis, Glen S. Douthit, Doris M. Drury, Michael H. Feinstein, Judith B. Foster, Betty Freedman, Beverly Martinez Grall, Carol Green, Donna M. Hamilton, S. Gail Hawkins, Janet Jackson, Norma E. Jones, Doris F. Ladd, Lorrena M. Lamb, June A. Larson, Joanne M. Lawrence, Sally Lazar, Dore Leiser, Brooke A. McMillin, Vercile Miller, Edna W. Mosley, Loretta M. Norgren, Myrte J. Oriel, Martha B. Perry, Ruth Ann Polidori, Fern Portnoy, Mildred Pomerantz, Virginia L. Razee, Alice G. Reynolds, Leah Rottman, Elaine R. Samuels, Gail S. Schoettler, Juereta P. Smith, Barbara Sudler, Alida Talmage, Carol N. Thomas, George Ann Victor, Doris White, Jo Anne Whiting, James O. Wilbanks, and Orion M. Wilbanks. Though it was impossible to tell each story and anecdote in depth, the subject matter is rich with potential and remains ripe for cultivation. For anyone wanting to take it further, I say cheers, tag, and you're it!

Please, each of you, believe me. The pleasure is always and forever mine.

GLW

ABOUT THE AUTHOR

Photo © 2017 Dan D'Errico

Grace L. Williams is a financial media professional, insider trading expert, and accidental feminism and economics scholar. Her writing has been featured in *Forbes*, the *Wall Street Journal*, *Barron's*, *Harvard Business Review*, *Financial Advisor IQ*, and *RIA Intel*, among many others.